Thumbs Out!

Hitchhiking Around the World in 1970

Sally & Peter Blommer

Milwaukee, Wisconsin

Copyright © 2025 by Sally and Peter Blommer
All rights reserved.

Photos by the authors unless otherwise credited.

Maps created by Karen Cluppert, www.notjustwords.com

Published by
HenschelHAUS Publishing, Inc.
Milwaukee, Wisconsin
www.henschelHAUSbooks.com

ISBN: 9798998725227
LCCN: 2025937790

Printed in the United States of America

*To all the kind souls we encountered
on our travels, including
Bob Landman in Texas,
Mac Hathaway in the Yucatán,
my French Mama and Papa in France,
Nadir and Guillermo Teutli in Istanbul
The Afghan Rovers and
three German NGOs in Afghanistan,
KK in India,
Dr. Dickinson in Nepal,
Hiro, Linda and Tedsan in Japan*

*And in loving memory of "Weezie" —
Mary Louise Seaman Sandine*

Table of Contents

Maps

Mexico And Central America
    Mexico.. 4
    British Honduras 15
    Guatemala, El Salvador, Honduras, Nicaragua.... 18
    Costa Rica.. 25
    Panama 27

South America
    Columbia 30
    Ecuador and Galapagos 32
    Peru 42
    Bolivia 60
    Chile 61
    Argentina 67
    Paraguay 69
    Brazil.. 70

Europe
    Italy 77
    France, England, Germany.................................... 77
    Austria... 91
    Hungary 93
    Yugoslavia... 95
    Greece.. 98
    Bulgaria... 103
    Romania 106

Asia
    Turkey 109
    Iran... 126
    Afghanistan... 132

Pakistan	145
India	147
Nepal	159
Thailand	165
Malaysia	169
Singapore	172
Philippines	176
Japan	179
USA	188
Epilogue	189

MAPS

1. United States and Central America
2. South America
3. Europe
4. Asia

Map 1: United States and Central America

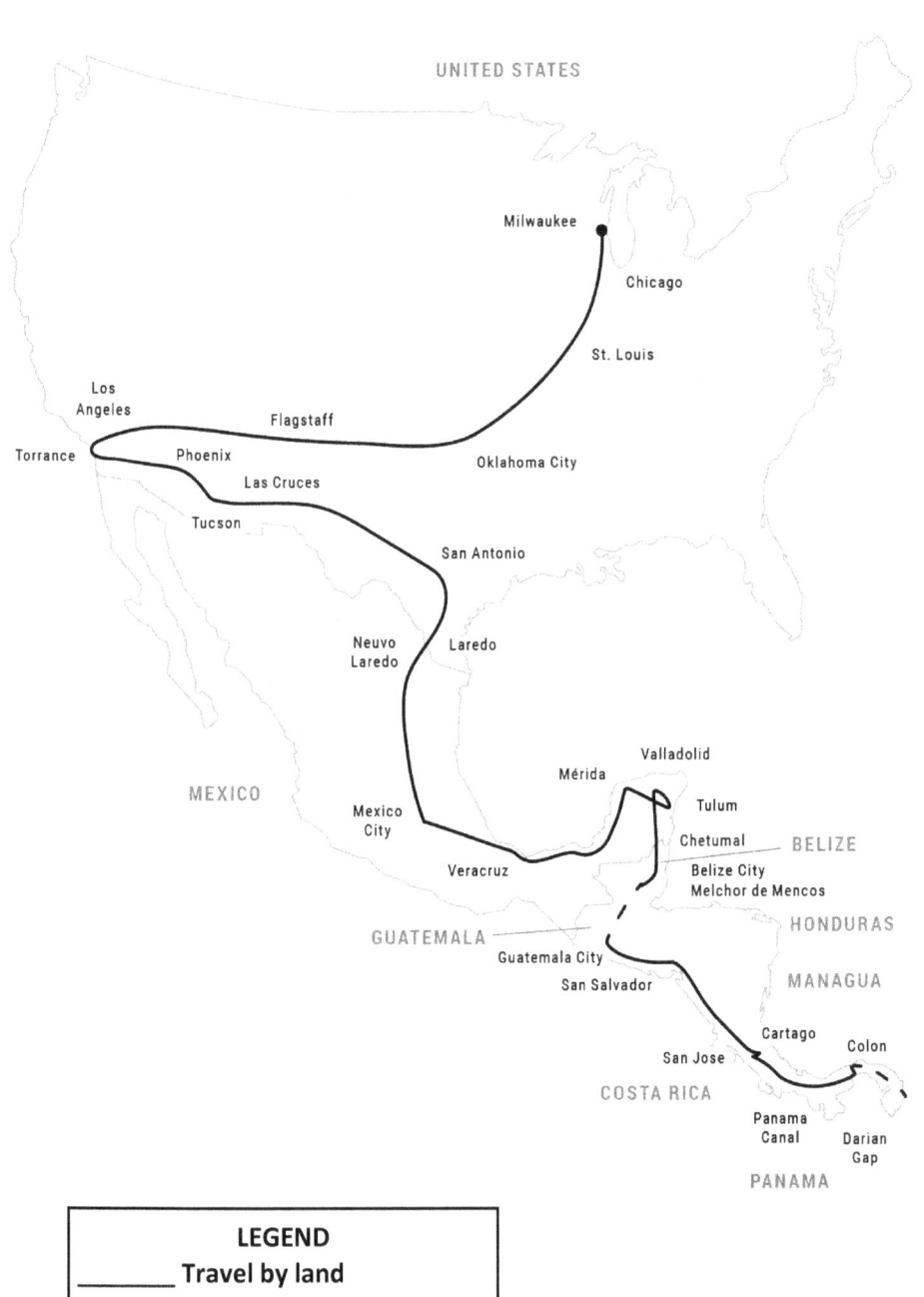

Map 2: South America

Map 3: Europe

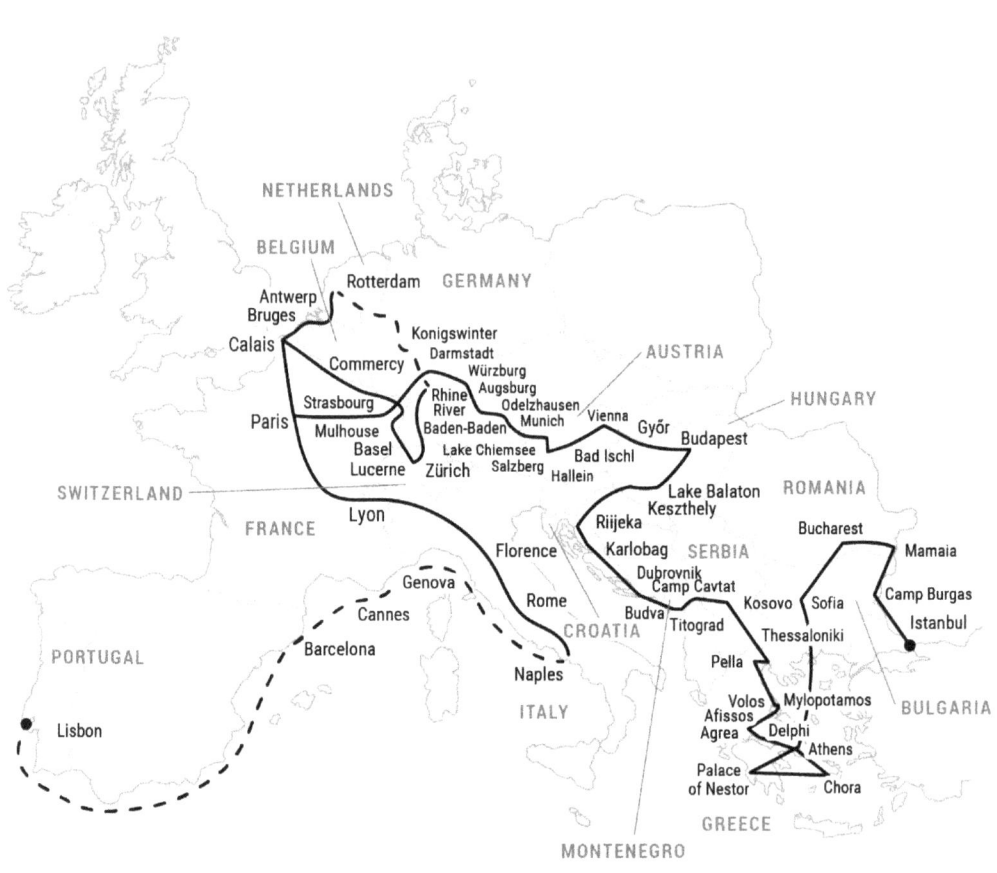

Map 4: Asia

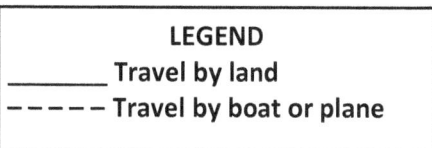

LEGEND
──────── Travel by land
─ ─ ─ ─ Travel by boat or plane

In September 1970, in a small village in Northern Afghanistan, we swelter in a lean-to tea shop. The landscape is barren, with light tan sand dunes. We can see for miles in either direction. There's not one motorized vehicle in this town. The men wearing turbans watch our every move as we scour the sand track for a smoke signal of road dust.

Peter tells me, "You know, sometimes you're a little too brave."

I answer, "I always think it'll work out."

+ + + + + + + + +

USA

We are in the University of Wisconsin-Milwaukee library, where we are auditing an evening World History class in the summer of 1969 for fun and a way to spend our time together. I whimsically spin an oversized world globe. "I want to go everywhere my finger touches."

"Me too," Peter replies as his finger joins mine—to travel around the world—lightly touching the globe.

Peter has always been a little part of my life. He hung around with my brother in high school. They were five years older and our house had the best fridge to raid. I've been out of school for a few years and Peter is living with three friends, including my brother, in a big, rented party house. He's been a postgraduate bachelor for seven years. So we think we know enough, and have been patient enough, to find a kindred spirit

Thumbs Out!

to live with for the rest of our lives. Soon we will be putting this to the test—we marry on November 29th, 1969.

On January 3rd, 1970, we begin our dream trip, an odyssey that will take us around the world, to the places we touched on the globe, and, following tips and instincts, to other places we haven't even heard of yet. We had decided not to share the details of our dream with anyone because we weren't sure we would complete our grand plan. We told our families only that Peter's goal was to see the Yucatán in Mexico and my goal was to visit the Galápagos Islands in Ecuador. With only this sketchy itinerary, our plan for now is to head south into Mexico then press on into Central America.

Peter finds a company called U-Drive, which pays us to drive a client's car, a black 1961 Nash Rambler, to Torrance, California. We bumble across the middle of the country, finding steaks for $1.59 and motels for five or six bucks per night. The only thing we could not find was a bar on Sunday to watch the Green Bay Packer game. We ended up watching the game in the lobby of a Holiday Inn. We drop off the car in Torrance and collect our cash fee for delivering the car—a whopping $125.

Our trip officially begins here. We walk the short distance to the nearest highway on-ramp and begin hitchhiking back east—1,500 miles to Laredo, Texas, and the Mexican border. We didn't think it through when we jumped at the opportunity to get paid to drive the car to California. We realize that this will not be our only mistake, but hopefully our only 3,000-mile mistake.

We share a single three-foot-long brown canvas duffel bag that Peter carries on one shoulder. We've folded and packed our clothes like folders in a file cabinet. When we unzip the bag, we see the fold of each item. My stuff takes up two-thirds of the bag, and Peter has the rest. Not knowing what awaited us, we attempted to pack for any occasion. Besides the necessary everyday shirts, pants, and socks, Peter has a blue sports coat and tie and I have an orange sundress. Every day, we have to work around this stuff to get to our functional clothes.

It's winter, so Peter is wearing warm tan corduroy pants. I wear a corduroy skirt and tall brown boots, and we're both wearing parkas. Our rides all the way to San Antonio are mostly pity rides—short rides from teenagers and older couples.

On Monday, January 12th, just outside of San Antonio, a shiny white BMW stops on the shoulder of the highway. The driver jumps out of his car and opens the empty trunk for our bag. He is in his mid-thirties, slim, taller than Peter, and has wavy black hair with pork-chop sideburns and a dark, thick mustache that curls down around his lips. He gives us a big smile. I like him instantly. He holds out his hand for a shake.

"I'm Bob Landman. Where are you headed?"

"Mexico and then hopefully South America," Peter answers.

Peter sits in front and I hop in the back seat. Bob tells us that he was in the Peace Corps in Bolivia for two years and lived in Mexico City for three years. We are all ears, sitting in on his Travel 101 class as we spin down the highway. His pointers are wide-ranging. "Don't hitchhike in Mexico. Transport is cheap there. If you have dollars, you can change them on the black market for a more favorable rate than the official bank rate."

Peter confesses, "We have traveler's checks. I thought it was a safer bet if stolen since they can be replaced."

Thumbs Out!

Bob continues, "No problem, you can change Traveler's checks for the same rate as dollars on the black market. You can get discounts at hotels when you mention the Peace Corps, which has doctors in the capital cities. You can call the US from any major post office in large cities."

Our travel education gets a boost from a veteran.

When we arrive in Laredo, Bob takes us to the Mexican consulate to obtain tourist cards for Mexico, then drives us across the border into Nuevo Laredo. At the train station, we confirm the departure time for the train to Mexico City. Bob then invites us to lunch and interprets the Spanish menu for us before dropping us back off at the train station later in the afternoon in time for our 3:30 train.

Mexico

While Peter buys our train tickets, I meet a trio of 20-year-olds—two clean-cut guys and a petite girl with a pixie haircut. They ask me to watch their luggage while they go to pick up their tourist cards. Later, riding south on the train, the boys show us their driver's license photos, where both had long beards to their chests and shoulder-length hair. They confess that they had to visit the barber before they could obtain their Mexican tourist cards. They're on their way to see the ruins of Tulum in the Yucatán. We know about the Yucatán—that's where we're headed. But this is the first time we've heard of Tulum. On the train, at every stop, we are bombarded by vendors selling food—oranges, sweets, and tacos made of mysterious meat. With a smirk, one of the reformed hippies opines that it just might be the meat of a dog.

USA & Central America

The next day, at around 8:30 p.m., our train staggers up over a pass and then glides down into a vast valley studded with twinkling lights, as if we are looking down at the Milky Way. Outside the chaotic Mexico City train station, we find an English-speaking cab driver who takes us to a cheap hotel near the city center.

> **Train: Nuevo Laredo, Mexico to Mexico City, 2025**
>
> The direct train no longer exists. There are several routes with bus and train connections. Mexico is now proposing a new route in the next few years.

On Wednesday, we are all business. Our first stop is the Guatemalan Embassy, where we apply for visas. We leave our passports to pick up the next day. Peter doesn't feel well and wants to head back to the hotel. We take a bus but get lost along the way. I thought he knew where the hotel was, and he thought I knew. We're learning our roles on the go. We finally get back to the hotel, where Peter sleeps all afternoon.

By Thursday morning, we're both sick. Early in our journey, we now face one of the many unknowns of travel: our health. We find an English-speaking German doctor in the city center. His speedy diagnosis is the Mexican flu. Our instructions are to rest, and we'll be fine in a few days.

We collapse on the bed in our stuffy, windowless hotel room, feeling depleted. It's a relief to have learned that we have the flu because we'd thought we might be experiencing psychosomatic symptoms brought on by our realization of how daunting this trip could be. We're newly married and newly on the road, so our strengths and weaknesses begin to show. I learned today that I need to be more vigilant about where we are and how to get back to the hotel. Also, look at the room before we commit to it and ensure we have a window.

We make a plan to debrief after destinations to decide whether or not it makes sense to press on. In our heads, we have a "Possible" file. In it, there's a memo to ourselves: *Circle the globe for a year*. Then we have a *Let's Be Real* file. This is the file we've shared with family and friends at home. Hopefully, after Mexico, we'll have our feet under us and then we'll lean toward keeping the *Possible* file open.

On Monday, we're well enough and antsy to get going again. Being ill, we never had a real meal in Mexico City, nor did we fully enjoy the city's attractions. But now we're anxious to see the newly opened Yucatán. We plan to leave Mexico City tomorrow. We pick up our passports and visas at the Guatemalan Embassy and get a required medical certificate from another office.

We leave the hotel early in the morning for the bus station. We're headed to Veracruz, then on to the Yucatán. The station is packed and smells like a backed-up toilet. I have many bad visions of a rickety old bus for the trip. A beautiful new bus pulls into the station just before 8:00 a.m., and it is ours! The bus is comfortable and air-conditioned, and we settle in for the ride.

After an hour, the driver stops for a break. Everyone piles out. We start a casual conversation with the two white-haired ladies who are sitting across the aisle from us. They are Dorothy, who goes by Dot, and Myrtle from Vancouver. They're headed to Tulum on the Yucatán Peninsula. We wonder, *Is everyone we meet on their way to Tulum, a place we just heard of?*

Dot tells us, "The road to Tulum is finally paved, but there are no places to stay." These ladies have done their homework and are a fount of information.

USA & Central America

At the next bus break, we ask them where they'll spend the night in Veracruz. Myrtle smiles. "Veracruz is our big splurge! We have one splurge on every trip. We will be staying at the Hotel Mocambo, an old colonial hotel just outside of town overlooking the Gulf of Mexico."

We arrive early in Veracruz. The ladies invite us to their hotel to have a drink with them at around 5:00 that afternoon and show us where to pick up the bus that will take us there.

We find an *hospedaje*, a basic low-cost inn. This time, I insist on looking at the room first to make sure it has a window. We clean up, then we ride the trolley that circles the city. We check out a few restaurants and pick a busy one for dinner. Later, we take the bus to Hotel Mocambo.

> **Veracruz, Mexico**
>
> As of January 2025, the Hotel Mocombo is still operating and is under constant renovation.

Dot and Myrtle give us a tour of the grand, old white villa, which was built in 1938 in a Spanish style with Moorish influences. We have a beer on one of the verandas facing the Gulf of Mexico. We don't see any other guests.

Dot explains, "We don't mind the lack of other guests. We anticipated this because it's the off-season, but we wanted to experience the grandeur of the past."

The ladies have been taking yearly vacations together for almost thirty years. They entertain us with details of the history of Veracruz and the conquistador Hernán Cortés, who landed on a nearby beach close by, 420 years ago, and burned all of his boats except for one."

Giggling, Myrtle says, "I don't think there were umbrellas on the beach then."

Thumbs Out!

The next morning, we meet Dot and Myrtle at the bus station. The buses to Mérida, the next stop on the route to the Yucatán and Tulum, are already full, so we buy tickets for the 3:30 bus, check our bags at the station, and head into town. This delay bothers Peter and he rues the fact that we didn't book the bus yesterday when we arrived. During a long seafood lunch, Dot and Myrtle share more of their knowledge of Mayan culture.

Our bus is late. This is what we were told to expect in Mexico and Central America. This is another thing that bothers Peter, and he realizes he will need to cope with these inevitabilities. At around 5:00 p.m., we finally set off on our 16-hour ride. I fall asleep on anything that moves. Peter likes to keep track of the driver's progress. I wake a few hours before we reach Mérida, as the sun rises, fields of henequen appear. Cacti fences surround the fields that have rows and rows of these magnificent plants, which look like giant, 5x5-foot aloe plants. At one time, the Yucatán grew 90 percent of the world's *henequen*, a source of hemp-like fiber. The plant is a relative of sisal that is indigenous to the Yucatán. The Aztecs and Mayans also made paper and cloth with it.

Midmorning, we check into an hospedaje in central Mérida. We both shower, then sleep-deprived Peter naps while I explore the neighborhood to get my bearings. There are many elegant, old Spanish churches and several large parks with towering trees. Later in the afternoon, I take Peter to the main square, where we meet Mac Hathaway, a short, pot-bellied replica of Hemingway. He's from Arizona, retired, and travels in his white VW van. He wears old blue jeans and a plain, used-to-be-white T-shirt. He's heading for the Mayan ruins and looking for passengers to share expenses. While we're talking to Mac, Dot and Myrtle arrive at the park. We call them over, and Mac invites all of us to join him on his trip to Tulum.

Peter and I say yes immediately. We look at the ladies, and they look at each other.

Dot's eyebrows rise, Myrtle gives a slight nod, and they say in unison, "Why not?"

The next morning, we all meet Mac in the square at 9:00 a.m. Peter rides up front with him, and we three ladies sit in the back. First, we drive ten miles north of Mérida to see the ruins of Dzibilchaltún, a city founded in 500 BC that had a population of 40,000 when the Spanish arrived there in 1541.

The people of Dzibilchaltún were salt traders who tended salt flats on the Gulf of Mexico that are still tended today. Many of the original stone buildings still stand. This site is near a beautiful *cenote*. Myrtle shares the information she gleaned from her Canadian guidebook about cenotes, or sinkholes. She explains that there are no rivers in the Yucatan. The landscape is what they call calcareous; it is covered with a layer of thin, dry soil, formed through a slow weathering of coral rocks. Rainfall trickles through and forms thin layers of water called aquifers. Aquifers flow horizontally and can form underground caves. When the ceilings of these caves collapse, a cenote appears as a small lake of freshwater.

From Dzibilchaltún, we continue to drive southeast to pay a visit to Mac's friend Hector, who lives in a small Mayan village on the way to Tulum. Mac and Hector met in the US and keep in touch by writing regularly. Hector speaks fluent English. He gives Mac a big hug and tells him how sad he was to hear that his wife, Marge, died a year ago. All three of Hector's children are curious and polite and, like most Mayan people, short in stature.

Thumbs Out!

Hector and his oldest son, who is about twelve, demonstrate their method of twisting henequen fiber into rope. Hector holds onto the ends of two bands of dried fiber while his son twists the bands clockwise. The henequen is slightly stretchy and extremely strong. They can weave in more bands as they go to produce a rope of any length. *Voilà!*

As we leave, Mac promises Hector that he will stop again on his way back home. We head to Chichén Itzá, the famous ruins of a large pre-Columbian city built by the Mayan people. There are no guards or fences around the archaeological site. Myrtle reads to us from her guidebook. We spend a long time here climbing up and down the well-preserved stone steps of the gigantic Mesoamerican pyramid-shaped temples, and exploring a cenote where virgins were said to have been sacrificed.

We drive past endless henequen fields and find a small store where we stop for dinner supplies. As the sun sets, we stop again beside the road. From here, we can make it to Tulum tomorrow. We pass by signs of construction and roadwork, but there are no hotels or villages in the area. Mac doles out blankets. He sits in the open side door of the van, and we surround him, sitting on his blankets. We put our food in the middle of our circle, and everyone makes their own sandwiches.

Mac tells us more about Hector. Hector was sixteen when he happened on Mac's house in Arizona, looking for work. Mac trained him to do auto repair work in his shop and gave him a small room above his garage. Marge, a teacher, taught Hector to speak English. They didn't have children, so they treated Hector like family. Hector lived with Marge and Mac for almost ten years before he returned to the Yucatán.

The sky darkens, and sprinkles of stars start to appear. Mac sleeps in the van. Peter and I find a place on a pile of small rocks that we attempt to smooth out, and the ladies find a spot across the road.

As I drift off to sleep, I hear Peter begin to laugh, "I love this shit."

A minute later, I reply, "Me too."

He continues: "Do you remember where we were six weeks ago?"

"Umm, Jamaica?" Peter lightly squeezes my shoulder and rubs my arm.

"Yeah."

We hearken back to the obligatory splash-out honeymoon trip we took to a posh resort on the beach in Jamaica. We both pretended to like it on the first day. By the third day, Peter said, "I feel like we're in jail." We requested an audience with the pompous British manager to propose our early departure and a partial refund. He agreed immediately, insinuating that our taste must be impaired not to be fully in love with his piece of Eden. We packed up and fled into the less well-travelled parts of the Caribbean, recognizing that we might prefer our now-seat-of-the-pants travel style to comfort and luxury. Now, we doze off in the Yucatán and sleep like rocks on our bed of rocks.

Sally on the stairs at Chichen Itza.

Thumbs Out!

The next morning, we are awakened by a construction crew that arrives in the dark, at 5:00 a.m. It turns out that the Mexican government is building an international airport for a yet-to-be-developed government-sponsored resort area that will be called Cancún.

> **Cancun, Mexico**
>
> Construction of the Cancun International Airport was started on January 24, 1970, and around 100 people lived in the area. The first three hotels opened in 1974. Now, in 2025, the population is one million, and there are over one hundred hotels.

We drive to an empty schoolyard, eat our breakfast, and continue past the henequen fields. In the small village of Puerto Dorado, we stop again for supplies, then forge our way south on a new highway for the last eighty miles to Tulum. It's a lonely road, flanked by sparce jungle, but occasionally, we catch glimpses of the Caribbean to the east. Finally, rising above the jungle, we see the white lighthouse of Tulum, which sits on a low cliff overlooking the blue Caribbean.

We head to the lighthouse, adjacent to the ruins of Tulum, and meet Ricardo, its manager. The lighthouse sits on cement pilings, and there are hammocks that we can rent, strung from piling to piling. Two other travelers are already camping here: George, from Oklahoma, who is sleeping in his truck; and an anthropologist, also from the US, who is studying Mayan culture and camping in a tent he's set up near the lighthouse.

We all get together for a bring-what-you-can dinner. The anthropologist brings tequila, which he generously shares, and tells us how Mayan calendars tracked the cycles of the moon. George tells us he came to Tulum driving his pickup truck through the jungle on small dirt tracks. He makes a yearly trip in his truck and has been traveling from one Mayan site to another in the Yucatán since 1963. He confirms that much is changing.

The ladies and I sleep in the hammocks while Mac sleeps in his van and Peter sleeps on the beach. I like to sleep under the stars, but the beach has too many critters scurrying around for me.

The next morning, Peter reports that he loved sleeping under a roof of stars. I'm becoming partial to hammocks. He and I spend the day exploring the Tulum ruins and swimming and walking on a beautiful, small beach nearby. Dot and Myrtle spend the day with Mac. In the late afternoon, Ricardo gives us a Spanish lesson before playing dominos with the anthropologist.

"Ricardo is showing off his Mayan excellence with numbers," the anthropologist says when Ricardo wins the game.

This has been a special part of our trip, exploring the Yucatán and the ruins and sleeping at the lighthouse of Tulum. In the morning, we sadly leave Tulum with Mac and drive inland toward Valladolid. We come to a crossroads and aren't sure which road to take. Mac, who does not even attempt to speak Spanish, finds a farmer passing by and asks him for *Vail loo did*. The man is perplexed. Mac asks louder. Finally, Myrtle pipes up with the proper pronunciation, which is *bah-yah-dol-leed* and the man points to the left road. We all poke fun at Mac.

> **Tulum, Mexico**
>
> In 2025, hotels stretch along the coast to Tulum. There is a fee to enter the antiquities where the lighthouse still stands.

Thumbs Out!

VW van with Mac, Peter, and Dot at the Tulum lighthouse.

We part ways at the bus station. Mac is heading back to see Hector. The ladies are taking the bus back to Mérida, and we are heading to Chetumal, then on to British Honduras. Our seat-of-the-pants plan, which we are discovering is our collective methodology, is to head to Guatemala and then hopefully Panama now that Peter has scratched his Yucatan itch. We simply assume there are roads and transport.

Our bus to Chetumal is packed with people, animals, and cargo. We are in the front and have a window seat on the seaside. Most of the trip takes us through the jungle. As we approach Chetumal, we see the Caribbean again. There is a cloudy, scarlet sunset sky with no rain but lightning over the ocean. Peter says the lightning creates the feeling of watching a slide show rather than scenery rolling past.

In Chetumal, we spend a sleepless night in an ant-infested hotel room that has a cold-water shower. Walking downtown in the morning, we both feel exhausted; we spot a taco stand and wait in a long line—a good sign—for breakfast. We hope we like British Honduras enough to spend a couple of days. Then we go to the bank, endure the usual long wait for service, and change our Mexican pesos into British Honduran dollars. We board a 10:00 a.m. bus to Belize City, the capital of British Honduras. Still in Quintana Roo, Mexico, we pass more of the region's characteristic oval-shaped, thatched-roof houses. Then we reach the border, where there is a delay while everyone gets off the bus to have their passports or identity cards stamped.

British Honduras (Belize)

In British Honduras, the route is straight, flat, treeless, lined with tidy, small wooden houses, brightly painted, perched on four-foot stilts, and covered with corrugated metal roofing. Red, purple, and white flowering bushes surround the houses. The clothes fluttering on the lines are vividly colored compared to the simple tan Mayan clothes we've become accustomed to.

Now, rather than the short Mayan people, we see tall, dark, slender people—descendants of enslaved people who were brought here from Africa by British settlers who relied on their labor to help them harvest timber, then sugarcane. The jungle is now replaced by farms with quaint names like Robinson Crusoe and God Bless Farm. Fields of sugarcane line the roads. Spanish is replaced by Caribbean Creole. British Honduras is the last surviving colonial outpost in

Thumbs Out!

Central America. It is bordered to the north by Mexico and to the west and south by Guatemala.

We are surprised by how high the prices are here compared to the Yucatán. Now we want to keep moving on to Guatemala, but we discover that there are no roads out or transport to Guatemala except back through the Yucatán. The Mayan mountain range and dense jungles separating British Honduras from Guatemala are roadless. Retracing our steps is not something we want to do; upon further inquiries, people tell us there is an airport where the road ends at Melchor, Guatemala, with cheap flights to Guatemala City.

In Mexico City a few weeks ago, we still had a feeling of trepidation, not nervous but we recognized our limited exposure to world travel. I grew up in a family of unconditional love leaving me forever confident. Peter was raised to be self-reliant. You get into trouble, you get yourself out of trouble. This turns out to be a good combination with lots of synergy.

Our goals are finite and limited. We mutually agree to set out each morning to proceed in the direction of a set destination, where new plans will have to be hatched, only vaguely informed about roads, terrain, overnights, food, climate, and transportation options. The big picture is seldom discussed until we find ourselves at our next point of reference.

Moving almost every day, it's impossible to know what's ahead of us. There is no doubt that an overwhelming obstacle could turn us back at any time. However, we are committed to inch forward to overcome barriers in the unknown. One step or ride at a time, and luck outweighs rationally informed decisions. Peter and I joyfully realize we are kindred spirits and embrace this unknown.

USA & Central America

To hitchhike southwest from Belize City, we wait in front of Jake's Filling Station and catch a ride with a Mennonite farmer who's heading inland to Cayo. He speaks English, Spanish and Pennsylvania Dutch, a type of German dialect. The farmer confirms that there are flights to Guatemala City from an airport outside of Cayo. He then entertains us with his family story of how they moved here from Mexico in 1955, a time when many Mennonite farmers left the country. Mexico was planning to impose a mandatory military draft, and because Mennonites are pacifists, they chose to leave.

British Honduras needed farmers at that time to help supply the country with sustainable food sources. So the government made a deal with the Mennonites—if they came to farm, they could buy land affordably and their children would be exempt from serving in the army.

The farmer explains that his farm is on a river with alligators, and the surrounding jungle is home to wild boars, snakes, and jaguars. We get the sense that this country is being ever so slowly tamed. He tells us that the majority of the farmers here are Mennonites. To us, they look like Amish people, with the same plain clothes, but Mennonites are willing to use electricity and tractors, which the Amish are not. Mennonites are not only expert farmers but also skilled carpenters and builders, our driver tells us.

We sleep in the only hotel in Cayo, a small city that exists to service the farmers.

The next day, we hitch an hour ride in the back of a truck to the airport, a dirt airstrip where the road ends next to a small grocery store/air terminal. The grocery store has a sign that reads "Melchor, Guatemala." There is no border crossing. We buy our two tickets to Guatemala City in British Honduran dollars, the equivalent of $14 US, and wait for our plane in the store. At around noon, an old DC-3 prop plane lumbers in. This plane was used in World War II to haul cargo, transport troops, drop paratroopers, and act as a flying ambulance. The workhorse DC-3 is the safest airplane ever built.

The cargo is loaded first, then passengers with animals' board, and finally, the rest of us climb into the plane. We have been issued no tickets, so our entry is obviously based on the fact that we are the only gringos. There are about twenty passengers plus animals and cargo. We sit on a long bench with our backs against the plane's wall. There are no windows except where the pilots sit. The plane is entirely open, with no divider separating us from the pilots. The cargo packed in the middle includes chickens clucking in baskets, a dog on a leash, and two goats loosely tethered together.

We make three stops, two of which are in mountain valleys. At each stop, all the passengers get off and wait for half an hour. We lose some passengers and gain others. Every airport has a simple shed with one or two workers who do all the work—helping with the landings and takeoffs and loading cargo. On our first stop, we can see from the airport a magnificent pyramid staircase that towers above the jungle. It's Tikal, an ancient Mayan city that thrived in the first millennium and is now enveloped by the jungle.

Guatemala, El Salvador, Honduras, Nicaragua

Our last leg is two hours long; we land in Guatemala City, with no border formalities and take a taxi into town. We stay at the recommended Chalet Swiss Pension, a family-run hotel. The prices are far more reasonable here. At the pension, we meet a couple from Kansas on their honeymoon. Tonight, in the temperate climate of the higher altitude, we sleep like babies under a light, Swiss comforter in our naturally cool room. The altitude of the city is 4,897 feet.

January 29th is our two-month anniversary. We sleep in to celebrate. The city is clean and easy to navigate. Today, job one is to change our remaining British Honduran dollars to Guatemalan pesos. We are turned away from every bank. The banks all have large maps of Guatemala hanging on their walls that show the area of British Honduras as part of Guatemala. The banks do not recognize the currency because the Guatemalan government does not recognize British Honduras as a separate country. Guatemala considered the area theirs and, in 1933, called on the US and Britain to resolve the dispute over it, but neither country wanted to deal with it. We even try to change our money at the British Embassy, with no luck. Finally, we inquire with the *dueña* at our pension, and fortunately, she knows someone heading to British Honduras who is willing to exchange money with us.

> **British Honduras**
>
> The name Belize was adopted in 1973 as a self-governing colony until independence in 1981. Guatemala's claims were dropped under international pressure.

This turns out to be our favorite city so far. We wander around town, Peter waves to get a person's attention to ask for directions and says, *Perdón*. Each person he flags down stops looks him in the eye, and reaches out for a polite handshake, saying, *Encantado de conocerle*, which means, "Nice to meet

Thumbs Out!

you." Peter repeats the phrase and asks in Spanish for directions.

Most people offer to take us where we're trying to go, but we insist that we can follow their directions. We crisscross the city, to get visas for El Salvador, Honduras, Nicaragua, Costa Rica, and Panama. The military runs the country, and there are soldiers everywhere. We don't feel threatened by them, just protected. Our dueña tells us that the military is fighting the communist guerrillas in the northern jungle region that we just flew over.

In the middle of the city, there is a one-acre relief map of the entire country, surrounded by a viewing platform. We walk around the perimeter. Of course, it encompasses British Honduras. After seeing the rugged Mayan mountains that separate British Honduras from Guatemala, we now understand why there is no way to get here except by plane. The relief map was created in 1905, before photos taken from the air could help to understand the topography, and we are so taken by it that we go out of our way to view it every time we pass nearby.

It is time again to wash Peter's now grimy corduroy pants. We buy washing soap and fill the bathtub with all our dirty clothes. We stand in the tub barefoot in our underwear, stomping on our clothes as if we were making wine. Most of our clothes are easy to wash, rinse, and wring. But the corduroys weigh so much when they're wet, we both have to lift and wring them together, twisting them as if they are henequen and we are making a thick rope.

One afternoon, we walk to a beautiful shady park, sit on a bench, and talk about our trip. We have a heart-to-heart assessment of our different travel styles. I suggest a few more layovers in places of interest. Peter regrets his quick temper,

USA & Central America

*Aerial view of scale model map of the Republic of Guatemala, Central America. (Shutterstock). The relief map is now **120** years old and still includes Belize. The scale is **1:10,000** but the vertical scale is exaggerated five times, with overly pointy mountains.*

which he says is just frustration about his miscalculations, but pleads that he's learning to cope. I react to his flare-ups, so I resolve to work on not letting this bother me. I propose more job sharing, with each of us taking turns writing in our travel diary. Peter is insightful—the big picture is what he sees—I see the details within that picture.

I propose a little higher standard of hotel, transportation, and food. It is a very reasonable array of grievances. Our plan is to spend time in cities we find interesting, but otherwise,

Thumbs Out!

keep rolling along. Our talk results in Peter taking over writing the diary for a mere two days, then passing this task back to me, never to write in it again. Nevertheless, he starts checking with me frequently when making decisions that affect us, and this has never stopped.

We go to buy our bus tickets to nearby San Salvador, the capital of El Salvador, our next layover on our way to Panama. Peter at least confers with me about the fact that the local bus is $6 less than the first-class air-conditioned bus. Since it's not that hot, we decide to save $6 apiece. So much for our agreement to travel with slightly higher standards. Despite my occasional yearnings for a bit more comfort, I'm finding myself adapting to traveling on the cheap.

Our bus leaves Guatemala City early in the morning. It's cool when we start out, so we wear our parkas, but as the bus descends to the coast, it turns very hot. The route is lined with sugarcane and bananas. It's a six-hour bus ride to San Salvador along the Pan-American Highway.

Throughout Central America, the buses all have names, such as El Rápido, El Toro, or El Tigre. However, since last year, when Neil Armstrong and Buzz Aldrin landed on the moon in Apollo 11 on July 20th, there's been a great wave of buses being renamed Apollo 11. It's become by far the most popular name, and it's the name of the bus we're riding in today.

After we arrive in hot San Salvador, we watch Apollo 11 pulling out of the station—and realize only then that we left our parkas on our seats. We set off chasing the bus, waving and shouting. A man tells us the bus will make its first stop not far from here. We jump in a cab and soon find the bus at its next stop. We retrieve our parkas and continue in the cab to find the recommended Hotel Bruno for a one-night stand.

USA & Central America

We eat bananas for dinner. Again, so much for the commitments made during our recent heart-to-heart.

In this heat, we decide to take the first-class air-conditioned TICA bus for the 17-hour trip from here to Managua, Nicaragua. The TICA bus company is an international operation that runs well-maintained, clean, and comfortable buses down the Pan-American Highway from Guatemala City to Panama City. They adhere to their schedules for the most part. Peter tries to make good on his commitment to find us more comfortable transport, but as luck would have it, our bus breaks down midway through the trip. The replacement bus we get on to complete our journey is older, smaller, un-air-conditioned, and packed. To stave off our thirst during this hot ride through endless sugarcane fields and cattle *fincas* (ranches), we eat the sweet, juicy oranges from the vendors who hop on the bus at every stop.

At the end of the day, we laugh at our trying to control our trip and realize that the vicissitudes of life on the road will continually bombard us. We need to swing with it and give up the consternations.

Leaving El Salvador, we stop at the border to pass through customs. We have to disembark from the bus and walk from El Salvador into Honduras. As we pass the border control buildings, we see fresh bullet holes in the walls, a result of the recent so-called Soccer War.

In July 1969, Honduras and El Salvador were competing for a slot in the 1970 World Cup in Mexico City, when long-simmering tensions between the countries erupted into open hostilities at the stadium and soon spread throughout the region. The Organization of American States arranged for a ceasefire after four days of fighting, but there were more than 2,000 casualties on each side of the 100-hour war, and some

Thumbs Out!

300,000 Salvadorans who worked in Honduras were displaced, expelled from the country, or forced to flee on their own.

These are days of zooming along, busing from capital to capital—none of which, after Guatemala City, seems to offer any compelling reason to lay over. After driving us the short distance through Honduras to the next border with Nicaragua, our rickety old bus pulls into Managua on a dark, hot, and humid night. We stay in another rat-trap hotel near the bus station, but it's just another layover stop for eight hours of sleep, and we do sleep.

Managua is a gritty city, so we're extra aware but never feel vulnerable. From what we're seeing, we're now hell-bent on getting to Panama, our next interim destination, where, after gathering information, we will have big decisions about what direction we'll head next.

We decide to get off the buses and hitchhike again, hoping for better luck. We get a few short rides, then a Nicaraguan family in a VW van picks us up. After a while, the father stops the van and asks us to get out with him. We're a bit confused by this. He takes us into a small restaurant and orders sandwiches and Cokes for the three of us. We eat while his entire family waits in the van. Because of our limited Spanish, our conversation is limited to *Where are you from?* and *Where are you going?* His behavior seems so atypical, since, throughout Central America, family has seemed to us the number-one priority. We continue with the family until they drop us off near the border with Costa Rica.

USA & Central America

Costa Rica

We cross the border into Costa Rica and set up to hitchhike. The three American businessmen we had chatted with waiting in the passport control line stop to offer us a ride. They are driving a black Thunderbird with Nevada license plates. We sit in the large, comfortable back seat with Fred. Jake is at the wheel, and Hank rides shotgun. They have business in Costa Rica but never tell us what they do. These three guys have taken this trip before and know the territory. They playfully tease each other, and we enjoy their company.

When we get to San José, Jake tells Peter their hotel has cheap single rooms. I'm told to wait in the car while the guys get four rooms. Peter takes our bag up to the single room. After delivering their luggage to the rooms, the men return, and we all go to dinner. Later, back at the hotel, the men need to spirit me into the building, since we booked a single room. We've all been drinking, so this bit of hijinks entertains us. The consensus plan is that the four men surround me, and we walk in together. There is no elevator, so to hide me, they surround me, walking up the wide staircase. We almost make it, but Hank starts laughing. The laughter and the ensuing shushing pulls the night manager from behind the desk into the hall, where he spots me.

"Stop."

We all stop and look at him with wide eyes.

"I have you fellows in four singles. We do not have more singles. So one of you will have to pay for a double."

Peter steps up and goes with the night manager to book a double room.

Thumbs Out!

The next morning, as an apologetic gesture, Hank buys us breakfast and we part ways. We take a bus up to see the mountaintop Ruins of Cartago, the original capital of Costa Rica and the country's oldest town. Given the earthquake risks, the capital was moved to San José in 1835. There's a panoramic view from Cartago looking down over San José to the sea.

We meet two Canadians and a Frenchman who are also hitching to Panama. A pickup stops for all five of us. It's cold high up in the mountains. We snake around endless curves on a rough road that carries us over the mountains, and eventually, we get back down to the Pan-American Highway, where we're dropped off.

To improve our chances of getting picked up, we split away from the group. Peter and I catch a ride to the border in a United Fruit truck. I have to sit on Peter's lap in the cab. After a while, we pass a water-well and the driver stops about 200 yards later. He asks Peter to grab the bucket behind him and get some water from the well for the truck. Peter hops out, shuts the door, and starts toward the well. The driver grabs my left hand and tries to pull me toward him. I grab the door handle with my right hand, open the door, and jump out. The driver didn't expect this.

I wait for Peter next to the truck, leaving the door open. This seems so preposterous that I almost laugh. I don't want the driver to take off with our bag. Peter comes back, and the guy pretends to use the water, tipping but a couple of drops into the radiator. I say nothing.

The border is closed for the night when we get to Paso Bueno. We meet up again with the Canadians and the Frenchman, our fellow hitchhikers. We eat together at a tiny café. There is no menu. We each get a plate with an egg, a small steak, rice, and beans for 40 cents. There are no hotels. The Frenchman disappears, so we find an abandoned school bus to sleep in and share it with the Canadians. It's a long, hot night with lots of mosquitos. I whisper to Peter about my encounter with the truck driver.

"Why didn't you tell me?"

"Nothing happened, it was ridiculous, and we needed the ride."

Panama

We cross the border as soon as it opens. It's another "United Fruit Company" ride day, and we get to Panama City around 5:00 p.m.

We find the Hotel Cristóbal, a large, old, wooden hotel that has seen better days. It's built around a three-story atrium, with all the rooms opening onto walkways that circle the open area. Opposite the front door, there's a wide, elegant stairway. We're on the third floor and have a view from our room that overlooks all the other rooms and the lobby. We are ready for a break and excited to explore our options.

As we leave the hotel for dinner, we run into a group of ten travelers who are slightly younger than us. They invite us to meet them back at the beach stairway at 9:00 p.m. A military officer on the street told them he would sell them weed and to meet him at the beach stairs, not far from the hotel.

Peter says, "Sorry, we have plans."

We walk out of the hotel. I turn to Peter. "That could be fun."

"No. It sounds like a setup."

"How can you know that?"

Thumbs Out!

"He approached them. They did not approach him. I don't trust it."

Exhausted, we eat nearby at a Chinese restaurant and go to bed before 9:00 p.m. The sound of pounding on doors wakes us up around 1:00 a.m. We peek out of our door. We see a military man with a squad of policemen moving down the opposite walkway, banging on the doors. A sleepy guy with tousled hair inches open his door, and the police turn to look at the military man. He gives a slight nod, and the police pull the kid out of his room. They round up everyone we saw earlier and take them away, presumably to jail. We go back to bed. I whisper, "Well?"

Peter murmurs, "I rest my case."

In Panama, we finally reach the crossroads we've been aiming toward and must decide where we'll head from here. We can look for jobs on sailboats going west toward Asia, or we can continue winding our way south to South America.

"It's easy to get a job on a yacht. I'm experienced," Peter reports. Seven years earlier, he landed a job on the *Double Eagle*, a magnificent 98-foot schooner from Newport Beach, California, simply by being honest: "I don't know how to sail, but I will do any job you give me."

The captain and crew, good people who were professional sailors, mostly motored along the Mexican coast, avoiding the arduous task of putting up the boat's many sails as they made their way to Acapulco. They were also looking for possible charters, so they always hauled up all the sails when entering a port. The *Double Eagle* was a spectacular sight with its white sails flying. When they moored the schooner, the fiestas would begin.

The most memorable fiesta for Peter was in the village of Puerto Vallarta, where Richard Burton, Elizabeth Taylor, and

USA & Central America

Ava Gardner had just wrapped up *The Night of the Iguana*. Of course, the schooner's crew was invited to the opulent cast party. What a life!

We go to the Panama Yacht Club and find a bulletin board where people have tacked up notices for job opportunities to cook or clean on boats heading west, but the dates of departure are long past. We realize that we could be here for weeks or months trying to get on a ship.

Our next idea is to slog through the Darién Gap, the 160-mile gap in the Pan-American Highway between Panama and Colombia. We actually look into this option for a day. As usual, I am willing to consider any plan, although very dubious about this possible way forward. I tell Peter, "I am open to a bit of risk, but there is a limit to my 'buy in' as we proceed. I am not a Pollyanna, and this is not a viable option."

"You're nuts," locals tell us. They explain that it's a six-week trip in small canoes with many portages. There's a big chance of getting malaria, running out of food, and meeting snakes, alligators, or robbers.

> **Darién Gap**
> This daunting stretch of roadless rainforest between Central and South America has become a main route used by those pursuing a new life in the US.

We agree that hiking through this jungle in Colombia is way too risky. Our decisions have become collaborative, fast, and usually right. We agree on the big picture. Neither of us craves the upscale. In fact, we feel it gets in the way of seeing the real world. We invariably want clean sheets, a bed with a mattress, and a bathroom with running water. We realize that, at times, it will be basic, dirty, and uncomfortable. It's a package deal, just like marriage.

Thumbs Out!

After weighing our options, we decide to continue to South America and fly over the Darién Gap to Colombia. Now facing a longer-term commitment, we chill for a few days. We spend the mornings in Panama City getting visas for Colombia, Ecuador, Peru, Chile, Argentina, and Brazil, the countries we'll probably visit on our trip, and we spend the afternoons sightseeing. We cross over the isthmus in the Canal Zone, an unincorporated US territory, to the city of Colón at the Atlantic entrance to the Panama Canal, and watch ships going through the locks. It's a marvel of engineering. This 51-mile waterway connecting the Atlantic and Pacific was finally completed after ten years of construction in 1914.

> **Panama Canal**
>
> The Torrijos-Carter treaty provided for the handover of the canal to Panama in 1977. After joint control, Panama took full control in 1999.

Colombia

On Sunday, February 8th, we fly to Medellín, Colombia. At an airport kiosk, we get a list of hotels and choose the Nuevo Hotel. We hop on a bus. A young man tells us he can take us to the hotel, so we get off the bus with him, but he soon gets lost. A police car packed with four cops stops and they offer to take us to the hotel. Three of the police sit in the front while we sit smushed in the back with our bag and the other cop. When we arrive at the hotel, one of the cops hops out to check out the hotel for us. He gives it his approval, and we check in.

South America

Medellín is an impressive city with well-preserved Spanish architecture. But we have no intention of staying in Colombia for any length of time, heeding the warnings we've heard about the country being dangerous, with warring gangs and drug cartels. We are constantly advised to take care and not to let our bag out of our sight. This is the kind of local information we've learned to pay attention to.

The next morning, we set off on the bus to Pereira, a seven-hour ride south from Medellín that takes us through the Andes. The people on the bus seem unaccustomed to being in a moving vehicle. The driver takes the treacherous curves up and down the mountains at full speed. Almost everyone on the bus is puking. They puke out the windows, on the seats, and onto the floor. We are in the back row of the crowded bus, sitting in the middle with our duffel bag on the floor. We can see the wash of vomit on the metal floor flowing toward us in the back of the bus as we charge up the hills, then reverse and slosh back toward the front as we race downhill. We both barely avoid joining in the vomit quorum. Finally, the bus levels off for a few hours, passing pineapple plantations as we approach Pereira. A dry, brownish crust covers the floor and, sadly, the bottom of our bag.

After an extensive clean-up and getting a good night's sleep in Pereira, we are back to hitchhiking. The mountain climate here is perfect for growing coffee, and we see crops everywhere in the highlands. The driver of our first ride pulls

---

Medellin, Columbia

In the 1980s, Medellin was considered to be the most dangerous city in the world due to heavy cartel activity. In 2025, it is actually safer than some US cities.

over at a roadside stand to buy us a cup of coffee. We savor it at the very source of the beans.

We continue to move fast as we work our way toward the border. We pass through Cali and Popayán. Then the traffic thins, so we catch a bus to Pasto. We follow a 2,000-foot-steep river gorge down to a valley and arrive at the Pasto end after eight days of rain. The town is a muddy mess.

The next morning, we catch a ride out of town in a truck, pass through the border, and arrive in Ibarra, Ecuador.

Ecuador

After a night in Ibarra, we continue to hitchhike toward Quito, with rides that take us across the equator and provide glimpses of snowcapped Mount Chimborazo. At 20,702 feet, it is the highest dormant mountain volcano situated on the equator. Peter remarks that he always wondered where the closest snow to the equator would be.

Quito, the capital, rests in a bowl surrounded by mountains and, at 9,350 feet, is the second-highest capital after La Paz, Bolivia. The city is graced with wide boulevards, huge, old Spanish churches, and beautiful, whitewashed Spanish architecture. We meet a fellow traveler who has just come from Guayaquil. He tells us about a narrow-gauge train from here, Quito to Riobamba, and another even more spectacular train from Riobamba to Guayaquil. His wise advice is to take this trip before the train goes out of commission since nothing is kept up here. He never went to the Galápagos because boats go rarely, and he didn't have the time to wait. Our style of travel allows us to switch on a dime, so we decide to leave the next morning on the train to Riobamba.

South America

This train to Riobamba is supposed to have spectacular views, but today it's overcast and foggy, so we see only gray fog all day and arrive in the dark. The town is small and we find a clean, cheap hotel downtown.

The next morning, the sun is shining, so we can take in the beauty of this old Spanish town with its cobblestone streets and old stone churches crouching below snowcapped volcanos in what's known as the Valley of Volcanos. We are lucky to book two first-class seats, for 50 cents each, on the 7:00 a.m. train that will slowly descend 9,000 feet from Riobamba to the sea-level city of Guayaquil.

This train track is a wonder of engineering and is widely known as one of the world's most scenic train rides. The aisles are full of people perched on baskets, some housing chickens. The roof of the train is packed with passengers. We see the bottoms of their shoes above our window. As the train curves down the mountain, we can see all the local people packed on top of every car ahead of and behind us.

The train isn't long—it has only six cars—because, near the end of the trip, there's a steep drop down an escarpment called the Nose of the Devil, which has carefully engineered zigzagging tracks. Descending the Nose, the train never turns. Instead, we zig slowly forward down a steep slope to the right, then level off for the length of the train. The train stops, the tracks are switched by hand, and the train zags down backwards, inch by inch, to the left, again leveling off for the length of the train. We stop, switch to a new lower track, and

> **Devil's Nose Train, Ecuador**
> The railway was severely damaged by heavy rainfall during the El Nino in 1997-98 and suffered from general neglect. In 2025, tours are being fitfully offered in some sections.

Thumbs Out!

slowly zig forward to the right. We repeat this nine times to reach the bottom. We bid farewell to the snowcapped Andes as we sink gradually into the jungle. We are fascinated by this marvel of engineering.

After this unique train ride, we arrive at the train station in the port of Guayaquil. We're pulled and pushed by the crowds getting off the train and clamber aboard a shuttle boat that takes us across the bay into the city of Guayaquil.

We're just breaking out of the crowd at the dock when a black pickup stops. Peter goes over to the cab, talks to a girl in the passenger seat, and beckons me to follow, tossing the duffel in the cargo bed. We get in the back seat. Elizabeth is from Guayaquil and she spent a year of high school in Indiana, speaks perfect English, and wants to help us because everyone in Indiana was so kind to her. She said the minute she spotted us, she knew we were from the US. When we get settled, Elizabeth asks what we're doing in Guayaquil. We tell her we're hoping to go to the Galápagos. She says, "I don't know anyone who has been there." She and her boyfriend drive us to the hotel they recommend, the Majestic.

The next morning, we search for a boat that takes passengers to the Galápagos Islands. We soon discover that the one we can afford is an Ecuadorian Navy ship that takes supplies to the islands once a month. To our good fortune, we find out that this "cruise," as the locals generously call it, leaves Guayaquil in four days. So we agree to "join" the Ecuadorian Navy when the boat departs on February 20th.

In the meantime, the sun is scorching in Guayaquil. All the sidewalks have wood overhangs, and everyone carries umbrellas to protect them from Helios. Yet rather than hang out in this steamy city of little note, we travel to a few friendly seaside villages nearby. Let it be said, there is also nothing to do except go to the beach and count the waves.

When we return to the Majestic Hotel in Guayaquil, a young boy shows up, bringing us an invitation to Elizabeth's wedding on February 21st. We hate having to decline and ask the boy to pass on our congratulations to the happy couple, but on their wedding day, we'll already be on board our ship, heading to the Galápagos Islands.

Galápagos Islands, Equador

The Ecuadorian Navy ship we board in the evening before our departure the following morning at 7:00 turns out to be an old WWII American Navy vessel. Because we booked late, all the private cabins are taken. The handsome captain decides that Peter can sleep with the male crew, and I can sleep with the female crew. These are two gymnasium-sized rooms, each with a forest of bunk beds and bathrooms large enough for an army (or navy, in this case). The fans below in our rooms will not be twirling until the crew arrives tomorrow. The rooms are sweltering and smell after antiseptic like a hospital, so we get permission to spend the night sleeping in two chaise lounges on the deck.

Ecuadorian Navy ship.

We settle into our chaises as the stars overflow the night sky, creating an undulating white strip the size of the Amazon. We look north. There it is—the Big Dipper. We look south—the Southern Cross. We can see both hemispheres at

Thumbs Out!

once. How can there be enough room for our Earth in this crowded cathedral?

We are woken in the dark by scurrying blue uniforms, and soon the glaring orange orb of the sun barges into the sky. Throughout the day, we make sure to always be in the shade. Our trip to the Galápagos will last eleven nights in all, with three nights out at sea, and three nights back, traveling 650 miles each way. While the ship and crew stop to deliver supplies, we'll have time to explore. We'll see four islands in all, none with hotels.

We finally leave Guayaquil at sunset, twelve hours behind schedule.

We find the boat's tourist mess hall. A jumble of passengers are already seated. There are fifteen in all, and they're from Germany, Britain, Ireland, Italy, Argentina, Ecuador, and the US. The two other Americans are Joe and Chris Burkey, a newly married couple from DC who will live on Santa Cruz Island for their two-year tour with the Peace Corps. We have lots of time to get to know each other, and we all have one thing in common: a great desire to see the Galápagos. After dinner, we all gather on the deck to scrutinize the sky.

When it's time for bed, we head to our designated rooms. I find my big dormitory almost empty. Only two women crew members are already asleep there. I discover a private corner and curl up.

Galapagos, Ecuador

1970 marked the start of organized tours after which travel companies brought in tour ships and yachts. Today, about 100 ships are equipped for overnight guests. There are also hotels on some islands offering tours and day trips.

South America

Then someone is shaking my arm. It's Peter, "I can't sleep in there. It already stinks, and it's packed with sailors hacking and farting."

He flops down on the bunk across the small aisle. I smile and close my eyes.

"Sal," he whispers.

I open my eyes and see his arm reaching and fingers wiggling. I put my hand in his for a good night squeeze.

I am seasick for the first two days and sleep most of the time. Peter spends his time on deck with the other passengers. I can't face food, so I'm happy to be alone in my bunk.

On the third night, we reach the first island, San Cristóbal, and I feel fine. Our first glimpse of the island from the ship is at 7:00 a.m.—a dark cloud hangs over the black, barren volcanic hills. It looks ominous. The ship anchors offshore. Only four of us ferry to the port in a dinghy. Peter and I make the trip with Keith, a 23-year-old English chap who has been traveling around the world for three years, and Horst, a 20-something guy who has been working in Guayaquil for over two years and is about to return home to Germany. The rest of our small band is waiting for the more interesting islands.

As soon as we're dropped off from the dinghy, Horst announces he is walking around the island. "See you later," he says, and waves goodbye.

Horst is gone before we can ask him a single question. Keith and the two of us follow a worn-smooth path over the black, rugged rocks along the deep sea. Soon, the sun is beating down; it actually stings. We discover a small beach cove and a patch of shade created by an overhanging rock.

As we climb down to the beach, we pass seals lying everywhere on the rocks. They don't even look up. There are

Thumbs Out!

large and small iguanas skittering all over the black lava rocks, unique because they are the only iguanas in the world that live in a marine environment. The stark beauty of the barren, craggy rocks and stubby bushes that dot them comes alive when our eyes adjust; we're able to spot all the creatures living here. They pay no attention to us; we are just obstacles, like the rocks they must navigate around. We're intruders in their world.

Keith entertains us with stories of his favorite places in the world. He also puts a bug in our ear about going to the headwaters of the Amazon River and air-hitchhiking from there back to Lima. We swim and are joined by bored seals, and when the sun moves to an angle that leaves us no shade, we head back to the pier. The first dinghy we take off in has engine trouble, so we return to the dock for repairs.

Horst shows up. The soles of his shoes are shredded from the hot, jagged rocks. He has wrapped his feet by tearing his long-sleeve shirt in two. His chest and back are burned bright red. The crew radios the medic on the ship. Peter and Keith give him their shirts for the ride back and make him drink lots of water. The medic later reports that Horst has third-degree burns and his feet are badly cut up. He never leaves the ship again.

On the next day, moored off of San Cristóbal, we stay on the boat, sleep most of the morning, and go ashore for a swim in the afternoon. On the ship, they show the same two movies every night—*Electric Man*, in Spanish, and an Abbott and Costello film in English with Spanish subtitles. We prefer watching the night sky with the other travelers.

We set sail again at 10:00 the following morning and arrive after lunch at Floreana Island. The ship parks at the dock. Peter and I get off and search for the house of the

South America

famous Margret Wittmer, a German immigrant who has lived on the island since 1935. She and her late husband moved here for the health of their firstborn son, and had two more children on the island.

A sign outside of a large yellow wooden house invites us in. She offers us tea and free German cookies. We sit on the wide front porch, at the edge of this small town, looking out at her beautiful rose garden. Mrs. Wittmer is short, strong, and speaks English perfectly. Her blue eyes show a twinkle as she entertains us with her stories of moving here 35 years ago. She also wrote an insightful book about her adventure, entitled *Floreana: A Woman's Pilgrimage to the Galapagos*. One other German couple was living here when she arrived, and it wasn't until after WWII that other families came to settle on the island. We could have spent days talking with this engaging woman.

We join most of our fellow passengers at a swimming cove for the rest of the afternoon. Today, we really swim with the seals, which are darting around us in the water, barking for us to toss them sticks. Peter and I take a break on the beach. We are lying on the wet sand, looking up at the blue sky, listening to the gay barking of the seals. Peter hears a whirl of water and feels a thud of something very heavy landing next to him. He turns to see a huge sea lion lying beside him. The sea lion has a wide, closed-lip smile and his eyes are closed. If the sea lion rolled over, Peter would be squished. I rest on my elbows to look over at this magnificent animal. The sea lion opens one eye, glances at Peter, and slowly closes it again. We leave him to his nap and return to the boat with the others.

On the next day, we head to Isabela Island, which is famous for its flamingos. We go in search and finally spot but one. We find another beautiful beach for a swim.

Thumbs Out!

That afternoon, we leave for Santa Cruz Island and arrive at the dock with enough time to take a walk around the small town before dinner. There are no restaurants, just a dry goods store, houses, and warehouses.

Sally on a tortoise.

In Santa Cruz the next day, we visit the Darwin Institute, which is funded by the Rockefeller Foundation to study biology in the Galápagos, carrying on the work Charles Darwin started here when he visited the island in the 1830s. It's a small building with large pens outside that hold many different turtles. One turtle is more than a hundred years old and it's so big that the staff invites me to sit on its back for a photo op.

After lunch, we help Joe and Chris move into the Peace Corps house where they'll live for the next two years. When we return to our ship, we see Jacques Cousteau's ship, the *Calypso*, tied up next to us. We meet Ron Church, an American professional photographer who travels with the world-renowned oceanographer, and he offers to show us around the *Calypso*. It's a floating science lab for conserving the sea and all its life-forms. Cousteau will be here next week. That's the

> ### *Calypso*, Jacques Cousteau's Ship
>
> It was a converted WWII Royal Navy mine sweeper. In 1996, the *Calypso* sank in Singapore Harbor. She was resurrected and a long process of renovation was started. She is currently (2025) in Turkey and will be on display in France when the renovation is finished, possibly in two years.

South America

story of travel: You should have been here last week, or next week will be better.

Ron points out a small sailboat, the *Dove*, moored in the harbor. Robin Lee Grahm, its skipper, is an 18-year-old on the last leg of a three-year solo sailing trip around the world. He's taking a week off before returning to California.

> **Robin Lee Grahm**
>
> We never met him but saw his sailboat. He wrote The Dove in 1972 and a movie was made in 1974. He left California in 1965 and was on the home stretch in 1970. He now lives in Montana with his wife, whom he met on the trip and married in South Africa.

We sail next to North Seymour Island to replenish our freshwater supply. We take a swim off the island, then our ship returns to San Cristóbal. We spend the last day of our trip on San Cristóbal swimming, then set sail at 8:00 p.m. to begin the journey back to Guayaquil.

For three days, all we see is blue water. We get plenty of sleep, and we start to feel restless. We have a farewell lunch with beer on the ship.

This unique piece of nature is a world wonder and we are all so grateful to have enjoyed it in its prime. As sad as we are that this adventure has come to an end, we are eager to get back on the road and see what awaits us.

We arrive in Guayaquil around 3:00 p.m. and immediately head from one ice cream shop to the next, satisfying our craving for cold and sweet. We board a night boat, the *El Presidente*, to cross the gulf to Puerto Bolívar near the border of Ecuador and Peru. I sleep in a hammock while Peter sleeps on a cot beside me on the boat deck. We are now looking forward to Lima, Peru.

Thumbs Out!

On Thursday, March 5th, we arrive at 6:00 a.m. in Puerto Bolívar and take a 20-minute bus ride to the border with Peru.

Peru

After passing into Peru, without any formality, we take a taxi to the nearest town, Tumbes, where we board a bus for our 22-hour trip to Lima. One mile outside of town, the police stop the bus for a routine passport check. Our passports aren't stamped, so we're told we must get off the bus and return to the border to get a stamp. We get our money back from the bus driver, leave our bag with the police at the Tumbes checkpoint, and hitchhike back to the border, where we make sure that officials properly check us out of Ecuador and into Peru.

Once our passports are stamped, and we are officially allowed passage into Peru, Peter recognizes a parked sleek sports car that had passed our bus from the boat early this morning. He says, "Let's wait." Peter finally sees the driver going to the sports car and approaches him, asking if we can catch a ride to the Tumbes checkpoint, and the driver agrees. I climb into the small back seat, and Peter sits in front with the driver, who speaks English. They hit it off immediately, so the driver invites us to ride along with him all the way to Lima.

After we pick up our duffel from the police, we set off with our new friend, Paco Ossio, a slender, tall Peruvian with dark brown hair and hazel eyes. He's been scouting the roads to prepare for a special race in April—the 1970 World Cup Rally—which will cover 16,000 miles from London to Mexico

South America

City. He hopes to be racing in this rally and will also be racing this Sunday in Lima.

Peter has followed race-car driving since he was ten years old. His father took him and his younger brother, Joe, to a Formula One race through the streets of Elkhart Lake, Wisconsin. Last year, while we were dating, we went to watch the Indianapolis 500 race. The boys in the front seat have much to discuss while Paco's heavy foot sits on the accelerator.

We can see forever as we weave speedily along the barren coast, the blue Pacific Ocean on our right. There are fishing towns all along the coast, but the Pan-American Highway doesn't go through any of these small towns and has virtually no traffic; nothing slows us down. We see a green patch of civilization on the horizon, and soon we're whizzing by, looking for the next green patch.

We smell one town we're approaching even before we see its green dot on the horizon. A dried fish flour plant in the town emits an overwhelming odor. This area is a stark contrast to the jungle and coastal roads lined with banana plantations that we drove through in Ecuador. With our race-car driver, we make what would have been a 22-hour bus trip in 14 hours, arriving in Lima at 11:00 p.m. Paco drops us off at the Hotel Roma, near the heart of the city, which he assures us is a good value.

We explore Lima for the next few days, wandering around, soaking in the beauty of the Spanish architecture and large, leafy parks. We find good restaurants where we discover South American cuisine—*ceviche* (Peruvian sushi), *aji de gallina* (chicken stew), *papas rellenas* (stuffed potatoes), and *pollo* (chicken) *empanadas*. I am partial to the omnipresent street food—sweet corn sprinkled with goat cheese.

Thumbs Out!

Following up on Keith's tip, we decide to stop by a travel agency to gather information about traveling to the headwaters of the Amazon. We need to get the name of the town where we can catch a boat to Iquitos. The town, we learn, is Pucallpa, and the river there is the Ucayali River, a tributary of the Amazon. As we are finishing up with the travel agent, a well-dressed businessman walks into the agency.

"Will it be a difficult trip?" we ask.

The travel agent says, "I don't know."

The businessman, a kindred spirit, pipes up, "If it isn't difficult, it isn't any fun."

On Sunday, we oversleep and rush to the racetrack but miss seeing Paco finish in second place. This was the reason we stayed in Lima and we missed it. Tonight, offered a chance to see an American movie, we sneak into the local movie theatre to see *Hello Dolly*.

> **World Cup Road Rally 1970**
>
> The rally started in London on April 19th and covered 16,000 miles, ending on May 27th in Mexico City. There were 100 participants. The European segment ended in Lisbon, Portugal and started again in Rio de Janeiro, Brazil.

On Monday, we are up and out on the road at 7:30 a.m. to begin hitchhiking. Our new route will take us east into the mountains of Peru, then north to Huánuco. Our first ride is with José, who is driving a Cadillac. We leave Lima, nestled in drab clay hills, and head up toward Chosica. We climb the entire way, taking in the gradual change from brown to lush as we continue through vivid green mountain valleys. When we get to Jose's destination, he insists on helping us get to our next stop and even offers to pay for a taxi. We convince him that his biggest help would be to get us pointed in the right direction.

An old, faded, blue Opel Olympia, made in Germany, stops for us. The driver speaks a dialect we can't understand. We call him Cat because that is the word on his painter's hat. The car rattles, and the driver's door flies open on curves but won't open when the car is parked. The car is packed with junk, so we squeeze into the front seat with Cat. The glove compartment door keeps flying open and hitting my leg. The route is up and up, with glorious views of snowcapped mountains.

Then the car just stops. Cat jumps out, grabs a tool kit from the back seat, and, without conjecture, starts taking the engine apart. He finally gets to some part deep inside, pulls it out, and cleans it with care. Then he puts almost everything else back in. He has one part left over. He looks at it, looks at the engine, shrugs with a little smirk, then throws the part into his tool kit. The car starts.

After we drive over the Ticlio Pass, at 15,807 feet, we start down and see clear lakes below. It's very cold, and we go through a short hailstorm. Mothballs bounce off the faded blue bonnet. Then, abruptly, the sun reappears, warming our descent. We stop for lunch. While we eat empanadas from a roadside stand, Cat fixes the glove compartment door by wiring it to the radio knob.

We have no clear communication, so we surmise Cat is speaking his own slang. Every time he stops, we expect that this is the end of the ride. Then he motions for us to get back in the car. Seven hours after he picked us up, he drops us off at a police checkpoint on the road.

After a while, a small VW Beetle stops to pick us up. We can understand this man's Spanish. Peter sits in the front. I'm

Thumbs Out!

in the back with supplies of aspirin and Bufferin. We call this man "Pharm" for the pharmaceuticals he sells. He makes a few short sales stops on the way and drops us off at 11:00 p.m. at the same hotel in the center of Huánuco where he's staying. He gives us a plentiful supply of aspirin and Bufferin for the road. We flop into bed with reviews of today's awe-inspiring scenery dancing in our heads.

The next morning, we drag ourselves out of bed and find the road to Tingo María. We spend an hour there on the side of the road watching drivers pass by, wiggling one hand, almost like the Queen's wave, and shaking their heads. Finally, a driver stops and explains that the road is closed due to the heavy rains of the last few days. We return to the hotel for a big breakfast and book another night.

We wander the city and meet two English-speaking Peruvian nurses who live in Tingo María. Their bus was canceled today, but they're confident the road will be open again tomorrow. They invite us to stay with them on their sleeping porch when we reach Tingo María, because, they explain, there are no hotels there. They draw us a map of the town square with an X that marks their house.

We get a slow start and leave around 2:00 p.m. the next day. A machine salesman picks us up in his VW Beetle. Peter is in front, and I'm in the back with the machine brochures. We have to wait for almost an hour to have the road crew clear the last blockage from the road. Then we make good time, even though the road is muddy and occasionally we have to drive through small rivers spilling across the road.

Tingo María is in what's called the high jungle, perched on an open plateau. The wide-open green valley hugged by the snow-capped Andes is stunning in the setting sun. We beat the nurses to their house, leave our duffel bag on their porch, and walk to town for dinner.

> **Tingo Maria, Peru**
> This was a tiny city with no lodgings, but now there are more than 20 hotels.

The next day, the nurses are up and dressed for work in their white starched uniforms. They inform us the unpaved road to Pucallpa, which was still closed yesterday due to the heavy rains, has been reopened. They give us homemade mosquito spray for our trip, and in return, we gift them aspirin and Bufferin.

We walk to the road after coffee and donuts from the street vendors. We realize that only trucks are allowed to pass on the soggy road. We pass up the open trucks packed with people standing in the back who are trying to get to Pucallpa.

Bruno, a barrel-chested, hairy truck driver, eventually picks us up. We can sit inside in the large passenger seat with him. His Spanish is indecipherable except for his ever-repeated mantra, *Vamos a ver* (We'll see). We have the whole day for this 12-hour trip to Pucallpa. Bumping along the muddy road, the truck soon gets stuck. It's magical how people appear from the jungle with tractors to pull or push us out. We then encounter an accident that stops traffic for five hours.

Once we're able to travel, Bruno decides to put more air in his tires and accidentally breaks off the nozzle of one of his tubes. He has to remove the tire to fix the tube. We now realize that we will arrive late—there is no other option. We finally get going again and follow a river through a narrow valley surrounded by white karsts towering above the green jungle. A full moon comes out to light the way. Resigned, we

Thumbs Out!

sleep on a tarp Bruno puts under the truck for us at 2:00 a.m., while he sleeps in the cab until 5:00 a.m.

Bruno drops us at the edge of Pucallpa at 10:00 a.m. We leave our bag at the local beer depot and find the only hotel in town, where we get breakfast. We meet Neil and James, two Brits who arrived from Iquitos last night. They are flying back to Lima in a few hours. They tell us the boat that leaves for Iquitos every ten days will leave today at 1:00 p.m. They're out of their room but still have the key. We gladly take up their offer to take a shower in their vacated room.

At 11:00 a.m., I head to the boat while Peter returns to the beer depot to retrieve our bag. It's all chained up, locked. He's directed to the owner's home, but no one is there. Peter returns to the depot and finds the owner's young son there, but he doesn't have the key. Tick tock, the time is now around 12:30 p.m. Eventually, the kid realizes we need the bag now. Peter helps the kid climb into a small window and then passes the bag out to Peter.

I am on the boat. The captain says we leave at 1:00 p.m., no exceptions. I close my eyes, trying to contact Peter in my head. At 12:50, I see Peter scurrying down to the pier with our bag. We leave right on time.

> **Pucullpa, Peru**
>
> The road is paved to Pulcullpa. There are more hotels than in Tingo Maria and boats go three times a week to Iquitos; the cargo boats are bigger now.

The boat isn't a passenger ship; it's a flat mini cargo barge. There's one cabin for the captain and crew at the back, the engine and the outhouse are in the middle, and in the front, there's a common area strung up with hammocks. This is also the area where they boil the muddy river water for drinking and cooking. It's covered with a metal roof to stave off the sun and rain. There's also an uncovered area where the cargo is stored. The cargo includes twenty aluminum boat shells being taken to Iquitos, and one of these boats becomes our cabin. The boat has a flat wooden floor. We stuff our bag in the bow and will sleep here for the next four nights. We use plenty of the homemade mosquito spray the nurses had given us in Tingo María.

The river is the width of a boulevard. We're heading downstream, with the muddy river water helping to push us along. The boat stays close to one side or the other, never the middle of the river. After a while, we glimpse one round thatch roof in the dense jungle, then a few more, and we arrive at our first village stop. The boat also serves as a mail boat, so we stop at each small village along the river to pick up or leave off mail, and it acts like a local bus. Sometimes, people board in one village and ride along with us in the boat just until we reach the next village downstream. In small villages, our stops are quick, lasting only about five minutes.

As the sun sets, the temperature quickly cools down. Tall, billowing cumulus clouds of pink and blue fill the sky, with rays of light shooting down through them. The jungle becomes alive with sounds. First, we hear the flurry of birds getting situated for the night, then the odd hoots, howls, and whoops of the unknown animals' nighttime conversations. We sleep listening to jungle music as our boat slices down the river.

We rise with the sun at 6:00. The boat stops at a larger village with a market. We eat hard-boiled eggs and bananas and take some fruit back to the boat. We buy some cans of soda since we just can't imagine bringing ourselves to drink boiled river water. We while away the day on the hammocks

Thumbs Out!

in the shade, watching the jungle glide by. In another village farther downstream, we meet a French priest and two nuns who have been spreading the faith here for three years.

After the third night on the boat, our backs are talking to us. We think one more night on this hard floor is about all we can handle. The river gets wider as we get farther downstream, and by the last day of our trip, it's almost a mile wide.

In Iquitos, the captain has everyone line up to get off the boat. He has a syringe in his hand and pokes the first guy with it, pulls the syringe out, and immediately pokes the next guy. We agree that whatever disease this shot is meant to protect us from, we'll take our chances instead of a high probability of contracting hepatitis from the shared needle. We get off the boat using a different gangplank. A young boy scurries after us to tell us the captain wants to see us. We go back to the boat and the captain asks if we paid.

"No."

"I understand you don't have much money, so just pay what you can."

Peter pays the equivalent of ten dollars.

In Iquitos, we find a decent hotel and, after wearing the same clothes for four days and nights, enjoy our long, hot

---

Iquitos, Peru

This thriving city is the largest in the world that cannot be reached by road. It sits in the middle of the Amazon rainforest. For a while in the 20th century, Iquitos became the richest city in Peru due to the rubber farms.

In 2024, Peru proposed and started construction of the longest bridge that eventually would connect Iquitos to the mainland. They built a 14-mile-long bridge crossing the Nanay River, a tributary to the Amazon. The indigenous leaders feel that this will change their way of life and ruin their habitat. The project is now on hold in 2025.

showers. We luxuriate in an actual bed and privacy. We are slow to get going in the morning. Around noon, we get up and head out to the airport on a reconnaissance run, remembering that this is where Keith, who we met in the Galápagos, air-hitchhiked back to Lima. We see a military plane on the tarmac, with stairs attached to its open door. We ask to speak with the captain, who comes out and tells us he doesn't have the authority to let us board his flight.

We begin the next two days by going out to the airport with our duffel bag all packed but end up returning to our hotel to check in for another night. We sightsee in the afternoons, wandering around the markets and docks.

On the third day, we see another military plane and ask for the captain.

It's the same guy we met on the first day. "Are you still here? I admire your persistence. Go to the military counter and buy the flight insurance so you can come on the plane."

We go to the desk and tell them the captain said we must pay the insurance to fly to Lima. It costs one dollar per person. We walk back to the plane, where the passengers gather at the foot of the stairs. A crew member starts shouting names to board the plane. Ours are the last two names called.

We arrive back in Lima at 4:30 p.m., take a bus back to the Hotel Roma, and are warmly welcomed back and given two bars of soap and a whole roll of toilet paper. We go to our favorite *salón de té*, where we savor the spinach pie and papas rellenas.

At night, we decide to go to the cockfights. The wooden arena seats surround an open circle in the middle. We sit way in the back because we think we'll get spattered with blood if we sit in the front. They put four cocks in the circle, each with a small, hook-shaped knife fastened to one foot. A smart, agile

Thumbs Out!

cock can jump up and slit the throat of another. If a cock keeps running away from the fight, the cock handlers clip its wings, so it has to fight. No one gets spattered with blood. There's a very active and complex betting system. We have no clue.

The next morning, we hitchhike out of Lima, heading toward the Altiplano, east then south toward Huancayo. We reach Huancayo in two rides. The first ride is with a man with one plastic hand. The next ride with a vitamin salesman who's traveling in the usual VW Beetle, takes us into the city. Again, I ride in back with the supplies.

Huancayo is the northernmost city on the Altiplano in the direction of Cusco in Peru. The next day, we head to Ayacucho. We catch a ride in the back of a pickup truck. We descend gradually through a green patchwork of plowed fields where every inch of tillable soil makes a design next to the steep rock cliffs. The air smells dry.

Eventually, cacti and yellow flowering trees appear. Then, with no more fields dressing the bare earth, only spare tufts of green grass poke up from the brown clay. Our driver drops us off at the university in Ayacucho, where we spend the night in dormitories for no charge. It is a large town in the southern Sierra region of the Altiplano. This high-altitude climate is harsh even in the summer and the nights are cold. We find some empanadas near the Plaza de Armas and go back to the dorms to sleep.

I awake around 5:00 a.m., alone in the girl's dorm. The roosters wake me in the dark with their false dawn cock-a-doodle-doos. I find Peter sleeping under a heavy blanket in the boy's dorm. He's ready to get up and get out. The dorms have cement floors and rows of bunk beds with no sheets. Dirty, cold, and built like a barn. Outside, we find the gate locked.

South America

Peter is helping me climb the fence when a guard comes and lets us out.

The night sky is still gloriously on display, and we see a comet streak across the sky. We walk to a nearby police control booth and wait till 9:30 a.m. to finally get a ride in an open-bed truck. I sit in the front seat with a lady and her four-month-old baby. Peter rides in the open back. His fellow travelers are barefooted locals fortified by chewing coca leaves, which bulge their cheeks and numb them to the cold, harsh environment. The coca plant supplies the coca leaves, which are also used in *mate de coca* tea, which we begin drinking regularly. The tea helps us survive the altitude and oxygenates the blood. The coca plant is also, unfortunately, processed into cocaine, hence the stigma against it.

The locals wear heavy, colorful clothes woven from the fleece of llamas and alpacas. These ubiquitous animals of the Altiplano are their source of milk, meat, and fleece. They also serve as reluctant beasts of burden.

Andahuaylas is 160 miles away, and we should reach it in about six hours. This eye-popping trip through the Altiplano is ever-changing—until we drop down into a hot, arid valley filled with banana and orange trees and get a flat tire. As the sun goes down, it turns very cold. The driver fixes the tire, and we start climbing again, but our driver stops a short while later at 9:00 p.m., in the middle of nowhere, to sleep. The lady with the baby in the cab and I try to get the driver moving again. He drives for another 30 minutes, then sleeps one hour. We arrive in Andahuaylas at 5:30 a.m. The nearly frozen Peter figures that the truck had averaged about ten miles per hour.

We head straight to the bus station, where we are thankfully able to catch a comfortable, warm bus to Cusco. Between

Thumbs Out!

naps, we take in a pink-cloud sunset over the Andes and arrive at our destination around 8:30 p.m. We check into the Hotel Plateros, take long, hot showers, then chow down on a tasty Italian meal at the nearby Café Roma.

We are perfecting our sign language skills. The people no longer speak Spanish but Quechua. The Quechua language predated the Incas, and the Incas adopted and spread it. It is the language used throughout these highlands. Quechua words we now know are *quinoa, poncho, llama,* and *condor.*

Cusco is the first real tourist town we've visited on this trip, and on Thursday, we start the day with *mate de coca* to help us cope with the city's high altitude—it sits 11,515 feet above sea level. We walk from the center of town, the Plaza de Armas, following the original Inca road through town, viewing the famous walls made of large stones that border the road.

It is a mystery as to how the Incas were able to build these durable walls without mortar. The huge blocks of rock in the walls are fitted together so precisely that you cannot get a razor blade between them. They are also built at a slight inward angle, which makes them earthquake-proof, a wonder of engineering.

The streets explode with bright colors. Men and women wear blankets that are a mix of primary colors, with red being predominant. They all wear blankets slung over one or both shoulders. Women in the highlands carry their babies in blankets on their backs, and wear long, bright, varicolored, heavy cloth skirts and abundant jewelry. The men carry brightly woven bags over one shoulder for coca leaves, slingshots, and stones to sling at anything that moves.

Even in the highlands, the men wear cropped pants and sandals with colorful braids crisscrossing their legs to strap them on. During the Inca period, there were state-run weaving centers where the fabric was woven. The best quality went to the rich, and had a 500-thread count—better than Europe could produce at the time. They used baby alpaca fleece, vicuna wool, vampire bat hairs, and hummingbirds' down to make the fine cloth. The fabric for the lower classes was made from llama and alpaca fleece and was 120-thread count. The Incas had a sophisticated and organized culture.

Here, the women wear their hair in two black braids, and the men wear their hair in a single black braid down the back. Men and women both wear small, felt bowler hats made from the fleece of llamas with colorful bands circling the crown.

The next morning, we decide to skip going to the famous nearby ruins of Machu Picchu in favor of heading toward Lake Titicaca and Bolivia. At 8:00 a.m., we attempt to hitchhike out of Cusco, heading toward Lake Titicaca, but there's hardly any traffic because it's Good Friday. We catch short rides to Sicuani. Then we get a ride in a jeep to just outside of La Rama, where our driver drops us off at the entrance to the Técnica Universidad Del Altiplano, a rural agricultural school, where he turns off.

> **Machu Picchu, Peru**
>
> In 1970, we decided not to go to Machu Picchu. The cost was US$14 per person and would have been a four-day commitment. The areas of Cusco and Machu Picchu are UNESCO Heritage sites and some of Peru's most visited spots.

As we soak up the warm sun, we are entertained by watching llamas grazing nearby, with the snowcapped Andes on the horizon. We drop our duffel down for a pillow. Our eyes close, then, after some ill-timed, brief naps, we hear the daily bus we're waiting for—rattling off down the road, away from us. There is no traffic, so we are stranded for the night. It

Thumbs Out!

starts to get cold as the sun sets. We open our bag and start putting on more clothes to stay warm. Not one vehicle passes by. We know it's about to get dark and colder. We now transition into survival mode, we decide that I leave Peter with the bag in the lee of a building and walk the mile into the university, where the jeep went.

I find a large, old Spanish *hacienda*. Calling this a university is a misnomer. This is a working farm gifted to the university as a place to study the animals and agriculture of the Altiplano. I enter the back door and start yoo-hooing, but no one answers. I go into a big kitchen, with wood piled against one wall. No one is here. I find a hallway and spy a door cracked open. I knock—no answer, go in. There's the boy who dropped us off sleeping in a small bedroom. I wake him and stumble through a baby Spanish rendition of "Husband on road, with luggage and no traffic, necessary to take the Jeep to him." Our Spanish, since we have been totally immersed in Latin America for a few months now, has improved. Not close to fluent by any standard but we are now capable of communicating our needs and wants.

The boy is groggy but understands, gets the keys for the Jeep, and we go get Peter. When we return, a woman is in the kitchen and has lit a fire to boil water. We drink hot coffee and are told we're welcome to spend the night. The lady takes us through the house, passing a large dining room, living room to another hall, a bedroom with a bathroom, and a large bed with sheets and many blankets. We put on adequate clothing and get into the bed, snuggling to get warm and wait to be called for dinner. It's pitch black in our room.

At around 8:00 p.m., a young boy, about 12 years old, knocks and invites us to dinner. He waits for us, holding a lit candle, then leads us through the dark house back to the candle-lit kitchen. We notice the boy is wearing a threadbare sweater, cotton pants, and is barefoot. We eat in the warm kitchen where there is a wood burning stove with the woman cook, the jeep driver, two men who apparently work here, and the barefoot boy.

We have soup, omelets, rice, and potatoes. We get an agricultural lesson from the group. Llamas are the largest, alpacas are medium size, and vicuñas are the smallest. The quality of the fur gets better as the animal gets smaller. Now, for the language lesson. *How are you?* in Quechua is *Imayna-yan kashanki?*

The next morning, we are up with the sun and take a tour around the farm in our parkas, long pants, extra socks, and, of course, our shoes. There are several men vaccinating the alpacas. We try our newly learned greeting and we get big smiles. We also greet a barefoot woman carrying a bucket of water. We marvel at her phenomenal capacity to withstand the bitter cold.

Back inside the kitchen, we have a breakfast of hot vicuña milk and alpaca meat that kind of tastes like pork. Then the jeep boy drops us off back at the road with our bag. We now know that we were looking at alpacas, not llamas. Soon we get a ride in the back of a small red pickup. The sun keeps us warm.

Outside of Juliaca, we finally spy Lake Titicaca. We can only see a small portion of the lake, surrounded by terraced fields. The lower fields are dotted with sheep. This is the highest navigable lake in the world. There's a police checkpoint outside the town of Puno. So the driver, a young man wearing a parka, gets out of the cab and asks us in perfect English for our passports so he can present them to the

Thumbs Out!

authorities. When he brings them back, he asks us where we're from.

As usual, we simplify: "Chicago."

"Oh, that's near Milwaukee, where I went to Marquette University."

Peter corrects himself, "Actually, we live in Milwaukee."

"My name is Roberto. Nice to meet you."

We spend the night in Puno. We walk down to the lake and spot an old steamship, the *Yavari*. A faded old informational sign in Spanish and English tells us the colorful back story. In 1861, the Peruvian government commissioned this ship to be built in Britain for use on Lake Titicaca. They had to divide it into 2,766 pieces like a puzzle. The total weight was 210 tons. The pieces were shipped to Chile. Each piece had to be under a certain weight so that mules could haul it over the Andes to Puno.

The *Yavari* was launched on December 25th, 1870, a century ago, and became the Peruvian Navy's first steel steamship on Lake Titicaca. The first problem, it was designed to run on coal, which was in short supply in the Altiplano, so she was converted to be powered with dried llama dung. Later, in 1914, a Swedish Bolinder four-cylinder semidiesel engine was retrofitted into the *Yavari* and she continued serving as a passenger and cargo vessel. Now, in 1970, judging from her dilapidated appearance, beached and abandoned, her time has come.

> **Yavari Ship**
>
> It is still around and is the oldest ship on Lake Titicaca. It was a museum for years and now is going through more renovations, with no date as to when it will be finished.

South America

On our way back from Lake Titicaca, we see a candlelit religious procession on the day before Easter. At the front, a man is carrying a large cross. Then, several priests pass in dark robes, followed by six men—three on each side of an ornate platform—carrying a statue of the Virgin Mary, dressed in black. A military band playing mournful music brings up the rear.

On Easter Sunday, fittingly, we get a ride with an American Franciscan nun who is driving a blue station wagon. She's on her way to the border between Peru and Bolivia. Margaret is from Minneapolis and, like Roberto, who drove us to Puno, also went to school in Milwaukee. We wend our way along the shore of Lake Titicaca. The lake is large, 95 miles long and 35 miles wide. Margaret becomes our tour guide.

We stop at a village called Llave and walk around in the indigenous market. We've now entered Aymara Indian territory. Their dress is similar to that of the Quechua. The women wear long skirts with banding of embroidery or velvet along the hems. The outfits are very expensive. One blouse and skirt can cost them the equivalent of 100 US dollars. Once purchased, the women wear these clothes daily.

In the market, the locals come dressed in their finest. They don't seem to care if they sell anything because it's their social time. They bring animals to sell, and, as Margaret explains, they usually return home with them. There is also a large selection of animal hides on sale at the market.

Next, we stop at Juli, another small village, to see an old Spanish church. Further south, in Yunguyo, there's an Easter parade led by men playing flutes, and by women in colorful dresses dancing and twirling. The locals harvest after Easter, so this parade is an expression of their hope for a good harvest. After the parade, they start drinking their homemade grain alcohol, hooch that they often consume until they fall down drunk. It's time to leave, and Margaret drops us at the outpost where we'll check out of Peru and enter Bolivia.

To cross the border, we must ride in the back of an official truck, where we're packed in like animals for the short crossing. People try to pile onto the truck as we get off, so we must push and shove. The border guards take an inordinate amount of time to stamp us in and check our bags for any smuggled goods. This checkpoint exaggerates the usual hassle that we've learned to cope with.

Bolivia

After finally crossing the border, we're the last two to board the bus heading toward La Paz, Bolivia. I am sitting to the left of the driver, next to his window, and Peter is sitting in the aisle on his right side, on a stool. Our route continues to follow the shores of Lake Titicaca, and we can still see the snowcapped mountains in the distance. The bus must take a short ferry ride to the end of the lake. As night falls, the bus dodges drunken Easter Eve celebrants weaving erratically along the roads. The driver is attentive and it's obvious he's dealt with these conditions before.

We reach the crest of a hill and look down on the sparkling lights of La Paz, the highest capital in the world, at 11,975 feet. Not having Bolivian pesos, we have an issue paying the bus driver, who won't bargain like we are used to. He finally accepts a US dollar. We check into a cheap hotel for the night.

March 30th is Peter's 30th birthday. We spend the day drinking coca tea to help us keep headaches at bay from the altitude. For this day and this day only, Peter reflects on his station in life while scrounging his way around South America on the cheap. He says, "You know, all my friends are advancing and pursuing their careers while I'm going nowhere."

I pull him into a hug, my head on his shoulder, "You're wrong. We are going somewhere—to see the world. And I know as well as you do that when we get home, you'll catch up in a heartbeat."

The next night, we board the night train that will carry us down from the Altiplano in Bolivia through the Atacama Desert to the coast of the Pacific in Antofagasta, northern Chile. It is the driest desert in the world. Rain is a rarity. This train will take around 12 hours to cover 700 miles.

> **Atacama Desert**
>
> This is the driest place in the world because it is sandwiched between two large mountain ranges—the Andes to the east and coastal mountains to the west. One-third of the world's copper is found here, as well as the largest supply of the world's nitrate. It is also one of the best places in the world for stargazing.

Chile

Early the following morning, we switch trains at the border, since we'll ride in trains that run on smaller gauge tracks in Chile. We have plenty of room to stretch out and sleep. It's gotten hot and dry as we leave the Andes. But we can't watch this barren Mars-like desert for long, since the unforgiving sun is angling right down on us and we have to lower our shades. Powerful gusts of wind pick up the tiny, speckled stones found in this desert and blow them like

Thumbs Out!

tumbleweeds. This dust forces us to close the windows as well. We arrive on the Pacific coast at Antofagasta around 8:00 p.m. It's a big town and there are plenty of inexpensive hotels.

The next day, starting towards Santiago, we take off early and catch several short rides to the main highway, still called the Pan American Highway. We get a ride in a big Mercedes-Benz delivery truck; we name the driver Benz in honor of his truck, which crawls uphill, but we can average 50 miles per hour on the straight flats.

Benz is a big, outgoing guy, but we can't decipher his Spanish. When we stop for food, he chooses a stand that sells live sea urchins. He buys two, pulls the live urchins out of their spiny shells, and pops them into his mouth. We decline and stick with bread and butter. Then, back on the road, the hills that the truck crawls up begin. At every stop, we think that we should get out and try for a different ride. But it's 10:00 p.m., and before we know it, it's 1:00 a.m. Benz decides to sleep. We try to hitch but have no luck in the pitch-black night on the cool coast. Finally, Benz gets going again, and in the early morning, we stop for gas.

In the gas station, we find a man driving a Fiat who agrees to give us a ride to Santiago. Fiat speaks to us in Spanish that's simple enough that we can understand him. We now have the first questions we are asked in Spanish down pat. *Where are you going? Where are you from? How long will you be here? How do you like our country?* When we answer, they think we speak Spanish fluently, so they pepper us with more questions and comments, leaving us both lost and silent but nodding. After half an hour, Fiat stops and buys us coffee and cheese sandwiches. He drops us off at the Mondada, an inexpensive hotel in the center of Santiago.

South America

Today, we go to the American Express office, hoping to get our mail from home. Generally, when we know our next big-city destination, we try to alert our family three or four weeks before we arrive there, so they can send us letters in care of the local AmEx office. This is how we stay in touch, even though these savored letters are usually at least three weeks old by the time we receive them.

In Panama, we had given our families a heads-up that we'd arrive here sometime in April, so we're pleased to find letters waiting for us. We leave the office and search for an upscale hotel, where we've heard that there's almost always one member of the staff who is willing to change money at the black-market rate. We get in the elevator with the operator.

Peter says, "Change money?"

"*Momentito*," the elevator operator says. He waves another couple into the elevator, drops them off, and then stops between floors.

He says, "How much? "

"Twenty," Peter says.

Then there is a short quibble about the rate. The elevator man won't budge, then gestures to indicate he's taking us back down, so Peter quickly agrees to his rate. The elevator operator turns his back as he gets out his Chilean pesos. Peter pulls our traveler's checks out of his pocket. He has one check for ten dollars and another for twenty. He looks at them both, signs the ten-dollar check and folds it. The elevator man turns to us, takes the check, never looks at it, slips it into his pocket, and gives us the equivalent of 20 dollars in Chilean pesos. He delivers us to the first floor, and we walk out. Peter then realizes he has inadvertently pulled off one of the oldest con tricks. We scurry home, thinking the guy will come to find us at any moment.

Thumbs Out!

The next day, we visit a travel agent and learn about Italmar, a cruise ship company with departures to Europe from Rio de Janeiro. We are just starting to investigate our travel options after South America.

Santiago is a grand capital, with well-preserved Spanish architecture, many large parks, and an old colonial feel to it. Santa Lucía Hill Park, with its park benches and expansive views of the city, ends up being our favorite.

We return to the travel agent to ask this time about tickets to Africa from Brazil. It looks like a short hop on a map, but there are simply no flights. We ask if there are ships that ply this route, but we can only find ships to Europe. We inquire about the Italian ship that goes from Rio to Lisbon, leaving on April 22nd. We think this might be our best option—maybe our only option, due to the dearth of departures.

We get back to our hotel to find our new friend, Mario, waiting for us with ballet tickets. Mario parks cars at a lot near our hotel, and we always chat when we pass by him. Yesterday, he told us about his love of ballet. I expressed an interest in the ballet, then he said he can get tickets to see the Ballet de Santiago. We've met some people on the road who tell us they'll come back later, meet us for dinner, or take us to the ballet, or the equivalent, but they don't come through. We've become skeptical, so we don't get our hopes up. But here is Mario with the ballet tickets in hand for tonight's performance. Our tickets are in the front row. We're so close we can't see the dancers' feet. We enjoy Mario and the ballet fully.

We've come to the realization that we'll need to leave South America from Buenos Aires or Rio. So we plan a new route south that will take us through the southern Alps of Chile and cross east into Argentina and the so-called Switzer-

South America

land of South America—Bariloche, Argentina—then head back north to Buenos Aires, or Rio de Janeiro in Brazil.

Before we leave Santiago the next day, Peter goes to a different upscale hotel to change more money. We set out to head south along the coast around 10:30 a.m., and we're soon picked up by two men in a spotless white car. We sit in the back seat. They both speak some English. They take short side trips to show us a waterfall and a special vista. We stop for a big lunch of steak, corn wrapped in leaves, and watermelon, and the two men drink two bottles of wine.

Chile is politically polarized, split almost 50/50 left and right, and an election is approaching. *In vino veritas*, they've loosened up and begin to rant to us about how bad the US is and how much they admire Russia. They drop us near the city of Los Angeles, about six hours south of Santiago.

Our next ride is in a spiffy Land Rover. The driver is a Chilean senator who speaks English and is on his way to take a break at his hunting lodge. He's wearing a stylish tweed jacket, and we can tell he's connected. As soon as he understands we're Americans, he forgoes the usual questions and abruptly asks, "Are you communists?"

We are stunned into silence. "No," we answer in unison after we recover. He then gives us his take on the upcoming election, in which Salvador Allende, a communist, has a very good chance of winning. The senator is vehemently opposed to Allende, so now we've been presented with both sides of the political divide. He takes us to Temuco, another two-hour drive south down the Pan-American Highway, and tries first to drop us off at an expensive hotel. We demur. Finally, after several attempts to find us an acceptably cheap hotel, he goes into the next hotel, presumably throwing his weight around and convincing the clerk to give us a room for a special low price.

Thumbs Out!

> **Salvador Allende**
>
> He was the first Marxist elected in a liberal democracy and served as president of Chile from November 3, 1970 to September 11, 1973. On that date, General Pinochet overthrew Allende's government. Allende died by "suicide."

Peter says, "That was a duly elected national senator who just drove us here." We ask ourselves why it's been so easy for us to hitch. And if it's so easy, why aren't there crowds of hitchhikers on these roads? The cars we ride in are far faster, safer, and more comfortable than the buses. These drivers have to make up their minds to pick us up in a split second. Upon reflection, we determine that our advantage is that we are a couple, so don't pose a threat and we look decent.

An innkeeper in Central America shared his observation of us: "Most of the young travelers passing through here are so raggedy. The two of you look so…so—looking for the right word—decent." I guess you would call us clean-cut. Peter has short hair and shaves. We both wear collared shirts and long, clean pants. It's advantageous for us to be clean and presentable as we're sticking out our thumbs.

As we leave Temuco, the traffic is light. We have a long wait on the highway to find a ride to Pucón, a city on the eastern shore of Lake Villarrica, about sixty miles south of here. In the late morning, a yellow Chevy Camaro stops. The driver is Stan Wilson, an American who works for NASA in Santiago. He is traveling with his Chilean girlfriend, My. They're on vacation and going to Bariloche, Argentina, as are we, and they invite us to join them for the trip.

We make a short stop at a store in Pucón for wine and empanadas, then drive on for a while more before stopping for a picnic. Stan is slight and thin, with blue eyes and sandy hair. My is petite, with short, black, styled hair. My has personality; she keeps the conversation going, and Stan, the scientist, speaks when he knows the answers.

Stan turns east into the mountains to an area famous for its *termas* (hot springs) and sulfur baths. We stop here for the night and head first to the baths. Peter overlooks that he is allergic to sulfur. He makes it to our room before a reaction kicks in and goes straight to bed. I don't like leaving him, but he insists that I give him space and time and he will be fine in the morning. I join Stan and My for a roasted lamb and wine dinner.

Argentina

The next morning, Peter has recovered, and the four of us press on toward Argentina. The Chilean landscape reminds us of Colorado. The road ends at a lake where a barge operating as a car ferry carries us across the water, after which we continue in Argentina through dry mountain scenery to San Carlos de Bariloche. Stan and My drop us off in Bariloche, which sits beside a clear blue lake named Nahuel Huapi and reminds us of a Swiss village surrounded by snowcapped mountains. We find a great deal at a higher-standard hotel. Later, we join Stan and My for our first Argentinean steak dinner, which does not disappoint.

We find a German-style deli with cheeses and sausages that keep us sated for days. It's owned by a middle-aged German man who speaks perfect English, Spanish, and Italian. He was in Italy during the war. *Hmmm.* His sons live in the US but he tells us he can't go there. *Hmmm.* At the end of the war, he, along with many Germans, including Nazis,

Thumbs Out!

escaped to Argentina. In Bariloche, we hear German as much as Spanish in the streets.

For our deli picnic, we take a bus out to the famous Hotel Llao Llao on Lake Nahuel Huapi, where Dwight Eisenhower is said to have stayed.

> **Chile to Bariloche, Argentina**
> This area is known as "Little Switzerland" and was notorious for all the Nazis who settled there after WWII.

On Thursday, April 9th, we head toward Buenos Aires, or BA, as it is abbreviated here. It's a long distance, more than 900 miles. We get a long ride, almost halfway there, in a truck that takes us to Bahía Blanca. We arrive late and having no guesthouses in the area, sleep a couple of hours on the ground near the highway.

The next morning, at 5:30, Ray Smith, an American, stops and picks us up in his blue Ford station wagon. We soon discover he's a contemporary of Peter's and went to Stanford with a friend of ours. It takes two days to cross the *pampas*. The word *pampas* is from the Quechua language, meaning flat surface; it might be expanded to mean redundant and boring.

We continue with Ray to his house outside BA, where we have lunch with him and his wife on their patio. Our first topic of conversation is the breakup of the Beatles. Then Ray, who travels on business, tells us about the new, huge Boeing 747 now in service and the French/UK-built supersonic Concorde plane. It's all news to us. We've been in our own little world while traveling in the big world. After lunch, Ray takes us to catch a commuter train to the city center.

In BA, we finally make our reservation for the Italian cruise ship that will take us from Rio de Janeiro to Lisbon,

Portugal, and we are set to sail on April 22nd. We are now on the clock, with only two weeks before we depart for Europe. We had understood the cost to be $340 for both of us, but we're now informed that is the per-person rate. On the bright side, we also discover that we can stay on the ship for six more days and continue to Naples, Italy from Lisbon, for just $5 more per person. We sign up for the bargain extended Mediterranean cruise.

Paraguay

On our way to Rio, we take a slight detour to visit Paraguay, a small, landlocked country with a population of 2.4 million. The attraction here is to get a feel for how the world was 50 years ago, since Paraguay has resisted modernization and the technological advancements that most other South American countries have embraced, and also to view the famous Iguazú Falls. Paraguay's president, Alfredo Stroessner, the son of German immigrants, took control of Paraguay by leading a military coup in 1954. He declared himself president and now rules with an iron fist. In 1967, he promoted himself again by declaring himself "President for Life."

We stay in the capital, Asunción, the only large city in Paraguay. Our hotel is on the main plaza, where there are no stop lights, and, even in 1970, there is not a single traffic light anywhere in the country, since there's so little traffic.

Paraguay's small population differs from the rest of South America. Most citizens are of foreign descent, and there are very few indigenous people. The economy here is agrarian, and the farms are owned and run by a diverse mixture of Mennonites, Japanese, Korean, and European immigrants.

Thumbs Out!

While we struggled to cash our traveler's checks in Argentina, here there is an open black market.

We take a five-hour bus trip to see Iguazú Falls, where more than 200 separate waterfalls form a U shape. We follow trails that take us to many different vantage points overlooking these spectacular falls, which are four times the size of Niagara Falls. The spray is refreshing, and the waterfalls are loud.

> **Ascension, Paraguay**
>
> Alfredo Stroessner served as dictator until 1989, 35 years. Paraguay now has a presidential representational government. The president is elected for one term of five years.

Brazil

From Iguazú Falls, it takes us three days to travel by bus from Paraguay to São Paulo, Brazil, where we board another bus that delivers us to Rio de Janeiro on Friday, April 17th, five days before our Italian cruise ship will sail.

We stay at a hotel in the Ipanema area and soon settle into a routine. Breakfast at the hotel. Sightseeing in the mornings, taking buses everywhere. Spending our afternoons on the world-famous Ipanema beach. It's the best body watching in the world, with all the beauties in string bikinis and the muscular men in Speedos.

We discover *Vitaminas*, a whirred-up fruit drink. Our favorite is made with avocado. We have at least one a day during our stay.

On Sunday afternoon, we attend a soccer game at Maracanã Stadium. The stadium is the largest in the world. It was built in 1950 to seat 200,000 spectators, double the size of

South America

most large stadiums in America. We buy cheap tickets, 50 cents each, so we're part of the loud and lively crowd. Drums are beating and oversized flags are waving. Soccer is a way of life in Brazil, and this is a typical Sunday game. The 1970 World Cup will start in Mexico City on June 21st, and Brazil is a favorite. Pelé, the iconic Brazilian soccer star, will make his last appearance there.

> **Maracana Stadium, Rio de Janero, Brazil**
>
> This stadium has been designated a national landmark, so no one can take it down. It has been renovated multiple times and the capacity has been significantly reduced to 150,000 from the 200,000 it originally held.

On Monday, we visit the Peace Corps doctor for complete physical exams, a safeguard after the exposure we've had to the different food, water, and germs over the last four months of travel. We return to his office on Wednesday, with our packed duffel, to get the results of our tests, and are relieved to receive a clean bill of health. From the doctor's office, we head directly to the ship—our home for the next 16 days—that will take us to Naples.

We're some of the last passengers to arrive at the ship, and with our lone duffel bag, certainly among those with the least luggage. Peter shoulders the duffel, and after we board, we're directed to a stairway that takes us down five flights of stairs. We find our cabin, 547, in the bowels of the ship. It has a bunk bed on one wall, with a sink and a small closet opposite; the bathroom we'll use is down the hall. We sidestep into the tiny, windowless stateroom, and I sit on the bottom bunk, pulling my legs up, to give Peter room to maneuver as he slides the duffel under the bed.

"We can live with this. This room is only for sleeping."

Thumbs Out!

"Let's go and explore the ship."

As we walk back up the five flights, I note landmarks so I know what door we need to use to return to our room. Peter, as usual, pays no attention to information he'll need to find his way back. We have fully assumed our roles by now, so this detail I know is left to me. We join the other passengers along the deck rail to have a last look at the famous statue of Christ the Redeemer, with his arms outstretched on Mount Corcovado, as the ship slowly turns its back on Rio and South America.

The Atlantic Ocean

A bell sounds. It is the first call for lunch. We have to go back to our room for the lunch pass. We follow the signs to the third-class dining room on a floor below the main deck. The dining room has no windows and there's one long table set up with lunch fixings in the middle, family style. Many people are already seated, passing plates.

A smiling steward approaches us and asks us to follow him. We follow him out and climb up to a deck that sits above the main deck and into a more formal dining room that looks like a restaurant.

The maître d' greets us at the entrance in English. "I was born in the States, and when I heard you speak American, I changed your table assignment to the second-class dining room. Your clothes are fine now, but in the evenings, Mr. Blommer will need to wear a coat and tie, and you, Madam, will need to wear a dress."

We are awarded a table for two at a small round window. Our waiter, Mario, serves our first lunch—typical Italian fare starting with soup. Mario is a small, round man with a big,

Europe

jovial personality. He's Italian and has been working on this ship for 15 years. He places new dining cards in front of Peter.

After lunch, we return to our cabin, and Peter picks through our filed clothes to find his long-sleeved shirt, sports coat, and tie, along with my orange frock. They've been filed for over a hundred days. The wrinkles have been perma-pressed into them.

That evening, we arrive in the dining room technically adhering to the dress code in our wrinkled and loose-fitting formal attire. Mario greets us, and there are smirks all around. We gaze out our window. It displays the lush blues and pinks of sunset over the calm, blue, endless sea.

Our first morning at sea, I get up early and go up on deck. Peter sleeps in. Just before lunch, Peter appears.

"Where have you been?"

"Lost." He grins.

His wanderings turn into reconnaissance. He found the engine room, the control room, the library, and the gym, and he discovered that our meal cards are a ticket to every amenity reserved for second-class passengers.

We are heading northeast from Rio to Lisbon, Portugal. Midtrip, we cross the equator. I'm so curious to experience the doldrums and the horse latitudes, patches of high-pressure calm in the middle of the ocean that occur on both sides of the equator. We learn that the doldrums are within five degrees on both sides of the equator and have moist air, while the horse latitudes fall within 30 degrees of the equator, on both sides, and have drier air. The horse latitudes' name comes from the early Spanish sailors who were often becalmed and were known to throw horses overboard to preserve food and water.

Thumbs Out!

As we pass over the equator, the winds in both latitudes are weak to nonexistent. For one day, the ocean is dead calm, with not a breath of wind. Our ship skates through, and the engine sings us along, leaving slow ripples in our wake.

Our days at sea blend together. Sleep, eat, repeat. I write in my diary, *Today, same as yesterday*. We enjoy the rest and the food, and we have fun with the South American and European passengers in the second-class lounge. We sit or walk on the deck for hours, reminiscing about our trip through South America.

To fill our lazy days at sea, we review our last four months on the road: the Yucatan, the train trips in Ecuador, the Galapagos, our ride with Paco, the Amazon headwaters, Stan and My, Bariloche, Iguazú Falls, and Rio. Reflecting on our first in-depth review with our cavalier planning, we look at each other.

I say, "What were we thinking? Are we nuts?"

Peter adds, "As Mac said in the Yucatan, I'd rather be lucky than to be smart."

I'm excited to get back to Europe, to reunite with my French Mama and Papa. I retell Peter about how I met them, whom I lived with for a month in 1966, and saw most recently when they came to our wedding in Milwaukee last November. While we went on our honeymoon, they traveled with my parents to Florida for two weeks before returning to France.

Some things just can't be explained. How is it that the usual perceptions can be so easily tossed aside? It is widely assumed that the cultured French will never embrace the down-to-earth, flamboyant American, especially a young, unsophisticated American. Four 20-something-year-old girls were blundering around Europe in a VW van on their way to

Europe

England. All the cross-channel ferries left from Calais, where we happened into the Buffet de la Gare restaurant for lunch.

My friend Smack picked up six full glasses of water in one hand to casually demonstrate this skill to us. The proprietor, Monsieur Clement Grimonprez, saw Smack's glass trick and jokingly offered her a job. Smack had a big personality, and I liked being her sidekick.

We thought it was a joke, but he said, "No, your English will be helpful."

"I want a job too," I chimed in.

The other girls wanted to continue to England with the VW van, but Smack and I stayed behind. I met Smack at a summer job in Montana at St. Mary's resort. She was my roommate.

We were never given any money but compensated with complete acceptance—plus room and board and the opportunity to live with the wonderful Grimonprez family. Smack liked one of the British waiters, Benny, and was consumed with him. Along with Benny, we lived below the restaurant in the family's home. There was Clem; his wife, Marie; and their three children—tall, heavyset Bernard, 19, studying to be a baker; beautiful, dark-haired Nelly, 14; and Arnold, aka No-No, the ten-year-old family clown and a clone of his father.

We started calling Marie our Mama, and Clem our Papa. Mama was short and round. She had curly, shoulder-length, dark hair, a beautiful face, and always wore dark dresses with a necklace and earrings. In her high heels, she was the same height as Papa, who was only about five-foot-four, although he seemed taller because he was very slim. He had thick, dark hair, wore glasses, and, always, a three-piece suit with a vest and a bow tie, his head held high with a closed-mouth smile and a twinkle in his eye.

Thumbs Out!

Our routine was to work the coffee machine behind the bar in the morning and take breakfast orders at the Buffet De La Gare (restaurant attached to the train station). For the rest of the day, Papa gave us French lessons, an education in wine, shared his interest in art, and described the French cuisine we enjoyed. We basked in the pure joy of being included in their family meals. One day, Mama decided she could take this opportunity to scratch her itch to visit London. Of course, Papa approved of this trip. I was invited to be her interpreter and companion. We shared a hotel room, visited museums and Harrods, and every day had reservations for lunch and dinner at the finest restaurants on Mama's "best of" list. Fortunately, all the waiters at these London establishments spoke French, relieving me of my translation duties.

Like me, Peter can't wait to see Papa and Mama again. Once off the ship, we're committed to a rapid trip to Calais. They know we are coming, but we could not give them an exact date.

After arriving in Lisbon and taking a walking tour of the city, we set off on May 1st to start our Mediterranean portion of the cruise. Many passengers disembark in Lisbon, and a new group arrives. Our ship slips through the gap between the Rock of Gibraltar and Tangiers, Morocco. Soon we are swallowed up by the Mediterranean Sea, with no land in sight.

But not for long. In each port of call—Barcelona, Cannes, and Genoa—we take four- to five-hour walking forays. It's raining when we arrive in Naples, our final destination, on May 5th. Mount Vesuvius rises in the mist above the city.

Europe

Italy

From my previous travels in Europe, I know that hitchhiking is easy here. When we get off the ship, we walk to the main road and catch two rides to central Rome. We find a room near the Spanish Steps and park our bag. I'm excited to lead Peter to all my favorite places, starting with Trevi Fountain, and then the Borghese Gallery to see my favorite Bernini statues. We also tour the Colosseum, which I'd missed on my previous trip. We walk out to the Vatican and find the Sistine Chapel is closed, just like it was when I was here before. We poke into any church that's open to see the artwork. We end the day with a delicious lasagna and pasta dinner, then sleep in a big bed *together* for the first time in weeks.

I had forgotten what it feels like to be surrounded by such a wealth of Old World beauty, culture, architecture, art, and cuisine. Our next stop is Florence, where we tour the Uffizi Galleries and stop to see Michelangelo's statue of David at the Galleria dell'Accademia di Firenze.

France, England, Germany

From Florence, we continue heading north and are now officially on our way to see my French Mama and Papa in Calais. We hitchhike over the French border and find a student hotel nearby to spend the night. In the morning, we walk to the highway, and a small, funny-looking car pulls over to give us a ride. I squeeze into the back with our bag, and Peter hops in front, ready to chat.

"Do you speak English?"

Thumbs Out!

"Yes, I went to medical school in the US."

"So you're a doctor?"

"Yes, I'm on my way to Lyon for the night shift. Where are you headed?"

"Lyon works for us. Our final destination is Calais. What kind of car is this?"

"It's a Citroën, but the cheapest model, which we affectionately call a *deux chevaux* (two horses). It's the French economical answer to the VW Beetle."

Peter thinks this car is a motorized tin can, dark blue with a canvas foldable roof. We bounce down the highway, never passing another car. It's an almost six-hour drive. The doctor and Peter have much to discuss, with the 1970 World Cup in Mexico City about to begin in June. The doctor is friendly, self-deprecating, soft-spoken, and seems to enjoy having company. I can see his happy blue eyes in the rearview mirror.

As we approach Lyon, the doctor invites us to sleep in his apartment. He hopes to get a quick nap in before going to work at 8:00 p.m., then, he says, the place will be ours. The apartment is across the street from his hospital. We enter the apartment, a fifth-floor walk-up, and the doctor sees the bare fridge. He suggests we go to the grocery store on the corner to

Deux Chevaux Citroen

AKA 2CV, which was produced by Citroen between 1948 and 1990. The joke was that it managed 0 to 60 mph in "about a day." In reality, it had a top speed of 40 mph.

Europe

pick up something for dinner. He'll leave the door unlocked while he naps.

We leave our bag and walk to the store for some groceries. The store is small, and when we check out, the clerk tells us he can't accept our traveler's check. There's a nurse in line behind us. She offers to take us to a bigger store after dropping off the milk she's just purchased at her mother's house.

While driving us, the nurse explains that the larger stores are outside the city center. Dropping off the milk takes time, then she drives us across town and proudly drops us off at a Super Store before driving off. There are 30 checkout counters.

We make sure they'll accept our traveler's check and begin our shopping. Then it dawns on us that we have to get back to the doctor's apartment. After traveling such a circuitous route to get here, we have no idea what part of Lyon we're in. Then we realize we don't even know the doctor's last name, his street address, or the name of the hospital where he works. We feel like we've hung ourselves out to dry.

We pick up our provisions and walk out into the large parking lot. We see a bus stop near the corner stoplight and head there. No one at the bus stop speaks English, nor do they want anything to do with us. The streetlights illuminate. We are growing desperate and decide to try hitchhiking at the stoplight. Cars roll down their windows in curiosity, but the drivers can't understand us. We know we need to get back before the doctor has to go to work.

Finally, a teenager rolls down his window. He speaks some English, and we explain that we're lost and all we know is where we're staying is in an apartment complex across from a hospital. He asks which hospital and tells us there are three. He says he can help us.

Thumbs Out!

Peter jumps in the back seat. I'm in the front. Our new teen friend tells me he just got his driver's license and is just driving around. He takes us to the first hospital. We immediately know this isn't it because there are no apartment buildings around it. Our driver is enjoying this misadventure with these bumbling Americans. The next hospital has apartments across from it, so we drive around it, and on our third turn, we see the doctor standing on his balcony looking for us. It's almost 8:00 p.m.

We race up to join the doctor before he sets off, and he bids us farewell because he knows we'll be gone before he returns home in the morning. As the door closes, we look at each other and shake our heads, realizing how close we'd come to missing the doctor. Our imaginations are overloaded as we both flick through the potential bad outcomes we just narrowly avoided. A bunch of small missteps had added up to a near disaster. We realize how well we team up when there is a problem.

In the morning, as we are getting ready to leave, the doctor returns earlier than expected and offers to take us to the highway out of town and drop us off. This is a big help since we have no idea where to go.

We get one short ride, then we're picked up by Sedan, a man driving a tan sedan. He has car trouble and needs to get a new fan belt. We stay with him while it gets fixed, then he takes us to lunch. Over lunch, he learns that Peter has never been to Paris, so he offers to make a quick side trip for Peter to see Paris. In the city, we all take a walk on the Champs-Elysees and see the Arc de Triomphe, then Sedan drives us along the Seine River. Later that evening, he drops us in Lille.

We catch a ride to Saint-Omer, then a spirited French boy picks us up and takes us the rest of the way to Calais. He's

Europe

driving another small Citroën Deux Chevaux, like the doctor's, and tells us that if he went to the US, he'd have to take this car with him because it is a very humorous car.

Peter says to me in a whisper, "This tin can couldn't even come close to passing the US safety laws and would never be allowed on the road."

We finally arrive at the Buffet de la Gare, a large, beautiful restaurant on the corner next to the train station. Since it's closed for the night, we find benches to sleep on in the train station next door.

The Buffet de la Gare opens at 6:00 a.m., and I know Papa will be there making sure the restaurant is ready to open, so we surprise him. Papa tells us about their trip to Florida with my parents after the wedding. My mother is short, like Mama and Papa. But my father is six-foot-three, so he towered over all of them. Papa got so sunburned that my mom made him wear a giant hat. He laughed recalling what a comical spectacle he made.

Mama joins us and pokes Papa to get going. She's excited to take us down the street. We have no idea what's going on. They lead us into an apartment building. We head up to the second floor, where there is a door with the name Blommer on it. Mama and Papa have arranged for us to stay in this apartment near the Buffet de la Gare. It's fully furnished, with two bedrooms and a kitchen well-stocked with French aperitifs and beer. We're invited to have all our meals with the family. This will be our home base for the next six weeks while we prepare for the next portion of our trip. We are flabbergasted at this generous gesture.

Three days after we arrive in Calais, we take the ferry to London to visit with Conway, an old friend we'd met in Milwaukee. Originally from Frankfurt, Conway is now living

Thumbs Out!

in London working in a bank. Since we decided to take the boat to Europe, our plans for traveling across Europe, visiting Mama and Papa in Calais, and, ultimately, traveling overland through Asia have gradually taken shape. Visiting Asia will require additional planning and preparations, so our London excursion is a nuts-and-bolts trip to acquire all the visas and inoculations we'll need to continue traveling east.

We start at the American Embassy, where we learn that some of the countries we're now planning to travel through in Europe and beyond before we reach India—including Hungary, Bulgaria, Romania, and Turkey—require visas for entry. We then visit the embassies of as many of these countries as we can to secure our visas. We also visit bookshops and libraries to research which cities and countries will be the most interesting to visit.

We don't only share a common language with the English but also appreciate the way they embrace world travel—so far on our journey, we've encountered intrepid Brits more often than any other travelers—and find plenty of resources in London. For the British, world travel is almost like a rite of passage. Often in Central and South America, especially in the remotest places, we'd cross paths with an amiable, eccentric Englishman. We heard a rumor about an English guy who was crossing South America on a horse, until his horse fell on him and broke the man's leg. We kept our eyes peeled for an Englishman in a cast but never saw him.

We return to Calais and, a week later, Papa and Mama decide that we'll take a road trip. Papa borrows a spiffy maroon Citroën sedan for the road trip, and Peter is our designated chauffeur. This Citroën is the most complicated car ever made. The independent, proud French engineers arrived at a design that is a complete automotive outlier. The

Europe

biggest difference from the rest of the world's cars is the pneumatic air suspension. When properly functioning, it allows these cushy vehicles to float down the highway, but it's a maintenance nightmare with too many moving parts. Papa sits in front, while Mama and I ride in the back.

Just before the Belgian border, Papa takes over the driving duties, since he's the registered user of the car. To get his eyes above the dashboard, we put a cushion under him, but it's still not high enough, so we add a second cushion, which elevates him just barely enough to see over the steering wheel. We start with a big jerk, then smoothly pass through the border with no formal registration check. One minute later, Mama vociferously insists that Peter take over the driving again, so he's back at the wheel, heading us toward Antwerp.

Papa has planned the trip around a few restaurants where he knows the chef or owner. We are always served the chef's choice and the regional specialty. Our culinary tour begins in Bruges, Belgium, then moves on to Holland, where we stop in Antwerp and Rotterdam. In Germany, we visit Duisburg, then spend two nights in Düsseldorf, where we drive along the Rhine and enjoy the region's special wines. From there we move on to Königswinter, then spend the night in Baden-Baden before touring Zurich, Switzerland. On day six, we lunch in Lucerne,

Papa, Mama, and Peter enjoying lunch along the Rhine.

Thumbs Out!

sightsee in Basel, and return to France, visiting Mulhouse, for the night.

On day seven, we spend time sightseeing in the Alsace region of France before arriving in Strasbourg for the night. The chef/owner of the restaurant where we head for dinner is a good friend of Papa's. First, we stop at the bar and enjoy an aperitif, a pastis served in a small champagne flute. At our table, a different wine accompanies each course. We start with a cold onion tart, served with a green salad with a simple oil and vinegar dressing. The main dish is *choucroute garnie*, a hearty local dish, and the *pièce de résistance* is *mousse au chocolat*. We end our meal with a digestif—Chartreuse, served on the rocks.

Not only does Papa know the restaurant's chef, he also knows the singer, a woman from Calais, who will perform tonight at 1:00 a.m. After dinner, we head to the theatre. Like most French people, Mama and Papa are broad-minded, so the fact that the show includes a striptease act doesn't faze them in the least, and Papa's friend sings well, making a great deal of eye contact with us. After all this, we realize it's now been over six hours since we parked the Citroën, and we can't remember where it is. We look up and down the streets. This sets us all off. We start laughing so hard that people walking past stop and help us find the car. The next day, we stop in Metz for lunch before arriving back in Calais at 9:30 p.m., dog-tired.

Not only are Mama and Papa a pleasure to be with and our generous benefactors, but Papa, even though English is his second language, is a wordsmith, and he can turn a phrase in an ever-so-colorful way. In Calais, Peter questions Papa's posted sign, "OFFERING HIGH TEA," in English at the Buffet, designed to beckon the numerous newly arrived

Europe

English tourists. Papa, with a smirk, explains, "It's a trick." Again, he entertains us with his creative choice of words for a sales pitch.

Peter and I have decided to buy a car, figuring we can tour more of Europe in it on our way to Turkey, and possibly drive all the way to India, where there is reportedly a market for second-hand cars.

We share our plans with Papa, who suggests we take the Citroën to Germany to buy a VW camper or van. Papa, suffering from his fear of sketchy border crossings, frets about our passing into Germany in a vehicle we don't own. After many phone calls, it's decided that a simple letter of explanation from the car's owner will be sufficient. In the Citroën, we sail across the border, with no ownership check, and continue to Frankfurt to search for a car. We are assiduously controlling our expenses, so we stay with Conway's mom in her son's now-vacated bedroom.

On June 14th, Peter heads to the local *bierstube* to watch the World Cup match between Germany and England, the team that won the last World Cup in 1966. The place is packed wall to wall with excited fans. Peter doesn't speak German but knows *ein bier, bitte* (one beer, please). Being in Germany, he is cheering on the home team. The bierstube is way too noisy to talk. The fans are yelling their game commentary, and Peter nods along, *ja, ja*. They assume he's German, even if he is a bit taciturn. West Germany wins by one goal, and Peter is back-slapped out the front door.

We begin looking for a VW camper van, but quickly learn they're out of our price range. So we buy a cheaper car, a 1962 tan VW Variant hatchback, from an American ex-GI who sells used cars outside a military base in Darmstadt, near Frankfurt. Mike McGee is all smiles and sees us coming. Later, we

Thumbs Out!

imagine his spotting us two know-nothings while he ordered his attendant to bring that car out from the way back lot for us. It was cheap, only $400, *but don't the Germans make the best cars in the world?* When it was new, this car was almost certainly a lemon. But now, well-used and eight years old, it's just short of the junkyard.

We return to Calais, Peter driving the Citroën, while I drive our secondhand Variant. It dies for the first time on the back street behind the Buffet, just before the restaurant's driveway. Papa comes out, and he and Peter push me in the car to the top of the driveway, which descends downhill from there, with a metal gate at the bottom. I can hear Papa's German shepherd barking behind the gate.

"Sal, you steer the car down, stop, then I'll open the gate. Papa and I will push to get you started."

I get behind the wheel. The car starts rolling and I'm furiously pushing the brake pedal, pumping it, but it isn't working. I'm gaining speed on the descent. I see Peter through the closed window. Everything is in slow motion. Peter's lips are saying, "Press the brake pedal."

My lips say, "I am. It's not working."

Crashing into the metal gate barely dents it—and our car also survives the impact. I realize now that I'd been pumping the clutch by mistake. Papa shakes his head, smiles at our ineptitude, and secures the dog. They push me into the garage. Papa reassures us that he knows where to take the car to have it checked out tomorrow.

We settle back into our Calais apartment. On Sunday, we head to the Buffet but the apartment door is locked. We are locked in. We need a key to get in and to get out, but we don't have a key at all. When we don't show up at the Buffet, Papa sends Nelly. We tell her through the closed door that we're locked in. Next, we hear the lock being jiggled. It's Mama, who

Europe

has come with various keys she has in her possession, but none of them open the door. She says she'll get a locksmith in the morning. Later, Bernard is outside the window calling up. He has a big basket of food for us from Mama and Papa. It takes several attempts for us to catch the rope he is tossing up, but finally, we haul up the basket.

The next morning we're awakened by the locksmith. He presents us with a key, and gives one to Mama.

We make one last trip to London to pick up our visas. We also get our second round of various vaccinations we received on our earlier trip to London. Now, being proud car owners, we must also procure car insurance and a *carnet de passage*, the red-tape proof-of-ownership paperwork we'll need to cross borders.

In London, we also visit a local pub with Conway to watch the final World Cup match between Italy and Brazil. We do miss the rowdy, enthusiastic home team fans here. Brazil crushes Italy by four goals to one. This is the third time they've won the World Cup. We're impressed by what an event these matches are over here, especially because there's still very little coverage of World Cup competition in the US.

Back in France for our final three days in Calais, we outfit our car with a spongy foam rubber pad for sleeping in the hatchback, and purchase two sleeping bags. Finally, on June 26th, we shove off. As a parting gift, Papa surprises us with our favorite cheese—twelve rounds of Camembert, scrupulously dated for *the best day to consume*. We have been wined and dined since the beginning of our transatlantic cruise on May 6th. Two solid months of splurging have given me a new gift of girth. My weight gain is evidenced by my newly snug-fitting clothes.

Thumbs Out!

From L to R: Peter, waitress, Sally, Mama, Nelly, Papa, and waiter. in Calais.

Peter says, "I thought women gained weight in their older years, not in the first six months of marriage."

He needed to say it, and I needed to hear it. So I commit to half portions of what Peter eats for a while. We figure that camping and making do with provisions from roadside markets will surely slim us back down. However, the real cutting back won't begin until we finish the Camembert.

Our overarching plan now is to reach New Delhi sometime in October and sell our car in India, then carry on by some still-to-be-determined route heading east from there. Our next big interim destination on the road to India will be Istanbul. It's a geographical pinch point, located on a triangular peninsula between Europe and Asia that bridges the Black

Europe

Sea and the Mediterranean. And fortunately, it is a must-see city. Our pace will be slow as we travel through Europe, since we want the scorching summer heat to dissipate before we reach Turkey.

Our car now gives us more flexibility and the tangential benefit of serving as our sleeping quarters. First, driving south from Calais, we return to Paris, where I take Peter on a day-long but more in-depth tour. We walk to the National Museum of Modern Art, the Eiffel Tower, and Notre Dame. We camp outside of Paris, enjoying our properly aged Camembert cheese and a fresh baguette for dinner.

The next day, it rains, and we follow small back roads to Commercy, which is about halfway to Darmstadt, where Mike Mcgee can make our VW right. We stop for dinner at a small, rustic inn before camping in the countryside.

We continue on the back roads the following morning, still in the rain, our car's engine groaning along. Finally, we cross the border and arrive in Darmstadt late in the day. Mike McGee couldn't be more generous about determining the cause of our car's bad performance, and Peter helps Manfred, Mike's mechanic, with the work. We spend three nights in Darmstadt waiting for our car repairs to be completed. We have enough time on our hands to buy a small gas stove and two folding chairs for camping.

After leaving Darmstadt, we continue heading east to Würzburg, in northern Bavaria, to visit Ingrid and Herman, a couple we'd met on our Atlantic cruise. We are invited to spend the night before my 25th birthday in their immaculate 150-year-old cottage in the center of this hilly city on the Main River. My dinner plate is surrounded by roses in honor of my birthday, and they give me a bottle of 4711, a traditional German eau de cologne. Inge serves up Wiener Schnitzel with

Thumbs Out!

warm southern German potato salad and special white asparagus.

When Inge and Herman understand we are heading to Munich and Salzburg, they put on their tour guide hats and recommend that we drive the Romantic Road, a popular route that passes picturesque towns and castles on the way to Augsburg. From there, we'll head east toward Munich and after we cross over into Austria, our hosts insist we not miss the Salt Mine tour near Salzburg. Tonight, though, we luxuriate in their hot shower and sleep in their big bed.

On my birthday, we follow the picturesque Romantic Road that's dotted with quaint, walled, Bavarian-style villages to the city of Augsburg, a larger rendition of the Bavarian villages we just passed through. We celebrate my birthday with a bratwurst dinner in a traditional beer hall in Odelzhausen. We finally find a farmer's field where we can park our car, and get to sleep at around 12:30 a.m.

From Odelzhausen, it's thirty miles to Munich, where, at the Marienplatz, the city's central square, we watch the 15-minute show of the Rathaus Glockenspiel, a giant mechanical clock. Then the clutch on our car breaks, and we spend the afternoon getting it fixed. This is getting so frequent that we take the long waits as an opportunity to explore any new territory.

After leaving Munich late in the afternoon, we drive about an hour and a half east to Lake Chiemsee, where we set up camp at an open spot on the lake. This is our first chance to use the new stove and folding chairs we purchased in Darmstadt. Having the car now also allows us to shop spontaneously for tasty, easy-to-cook dinners at any one of the ubiquitous small bodegas we pass along the way. We find glass jars of locally made specialties, already cooked. All we need to do is heat them up.

Our worries have been diminished, as we have no schedule and no transport contingencies. A routine sneaks in. Even the campsites are expensive in Western Europe, so we find secluded places to park and spend the night. A two-gallon plastic jug holds and supplies all of our water. We devise efficient ways to bathe using just one quart of water each. Then we fire up our stove and heat up our meal. We sit in our folding chairs, usually have a little wine, enjoy a nice view of the snowcapped Alps, and wait for our meal to heat. Later, we enjoy Papa's Camembert for dessert. In the morning, we heat water for Nescafé instant coffee, find breakfast or lunch along the way, and shop for more regional specialties.

Austria

On July 4th, we wake to rain. We have a thirty-minute drive to Salzburg. It's a city filled with tourists, set below snowcapped mountains, with beautiful architecture and window boxes heavy with colorful flowers. We get directions from here to Hallein, for the Salt Mine tour, another 20-minute drive away. There, we take a gondola to the top of a mountain, then walk down a steep path. We are issued white overalls and a white jacket to wear over our clothes. Then we're led to the entrance of the mine and have to walk about 50 feet before we see a wooden slide.

> **Hallein Salt Mine Tour**
> This mine is 2,500 years old and is still offering tours in 2025.

Thumbs Out!

Our English-speaking guide straddles the slide, telling me to get on behind him, put my legs around him, and put my hands on his shoulders. Peter follows suit, as do five other riders who board the slide behind him. The guide says, "Hang on." Then we fly down about a hundred feet before our guide brakes our speed using his legs and gloved hands to grip ropes on each side. We do this twice more, then we take a ride on a boat across a salt lake, take two more slides down, and finish up boarding a small, open train that goes through the mine and back out to where our car is parked. It's a thrill ride, and it's good to get the adrenaline flowing again. This thrill ride is something I like way more than Peter; he just puts up with it.

We return to Salzburg, then drive on to Bad Ischl, where, about six miles off the main road, we find a great camping place in a field on a mountainside. We cook soup and make hot chocolate and sleep. It rains again.

In the morning, the sun comes out, and we drive on back roads through the Alps via St. Michael. Everywhere we look, we see ski lifts, and below the mountains, there are spectacular fields of purple, yellow, and white flowers. In the afternoon, we find a spot on a wooded hill overlooking several small villages. The church spires rise above the tidy houses. We cook stew for dinner, take a walk in the woods, and collect a bouquet of wildflowers to adorn our car. We watch the lights go on in the small towns below, and then, above, the cover of a star-filled sky.

After waking with the sun at 5:30, we head to Vienna and arrive there around 8:30 a.m. The pastry shops doubly attract us with their oven aromas and mouthwatering displays. We buy a pastry for breakfast after a long perusal. Then we find the Hungarian Embassy, where we leave our passports in order to secure visas to visit Hungary. We drive to see the

Europe

Schönbrunn Palace, then out to the Vienna Woods, where we camp for the night.

Waking up again with the sun, we drive back to the city for coffee and pastry. Then, at 10:00 a.m., we line up to see the famous Lipizzaner stallions performing at the Spanish Riding School. The white horses are scrupulously trained to perform at a mere touch of the reins. Then we can't resist an apple strudel for our trip. We pick up our passports from the Hungarian Embassy and stop to pick cherries on our way out of town. We camp near the border.

> **Vienna, Austria**
>
> Lipizzaner horses are from Piber in Spain. This breeding farm has been in operation since the 1500s. They are trained in Austria from age four to ten to perform.

Hungary

We wake again at 5:30, make coffee, and eat our apple strudel. We drive out of Austria and into Hungary. We're surprised at how easy it is to enter Communist Hungary. There's only one glitch—our auto insurance does not cover driving in Hungary. When we're told to buy a Hungarian policy, we imagine a plot by the local cabal but at the insurance kiosk, they shake us down for a mere 75 cents.

Hungary is under the strong hand of Soviet Russia. The first thing we notice is how few cars there are on the road and how many bicycles and horse-drawn carts there are. We pass a large cement factory, and the parking lot is full of bicycles. We head toward Gyor. There are no farmhouses in the expansive fields. These are communal crops, mostly wheat,

Thumbs Out!

and the workers commute to them from the small, impoverished towns on bicycles or in wagons.

After Gyor, we follow the Danube River to Esztergom. Then we decide to stop in a rare restaurant in a small town. The prices in the restaurants are cheap and controlled by the government. We are seated just as nine Soviet soldiers come in. They look around and find a table. They demand vodka and order an enormous amount of food. No one in the restaurant is served until they are. They are rude, loud, and demanding. Everyone watches them surreptitiously. When they finish, they get up and leave, paying nothing. There was an uprising in Hungary in 1956, and the Russians squashed it with tanks and troops, which still remain.

> **Hungary**
>
> Hungary became independent in 1989. The transition was peaceful, and finally, thousands of Soviet troops left the country.

Monsieur Variant, as we've taken to calling our car, gobbles oil and frequently requires maintenance in VW service stations on our route. This francophone name is derived from the car's independent, almost haughty ways. The maintenance costs are taking a toll on our resources, and not even the cheap prices here can make up the difference. Food, gas, and supplies cost the same in every store. The jars of delicious homemade goulashes and stews we find here are dirt cheap.

We take a whirlwind tour of Budapest. Buda is on one side of the Danube, and Pest is on the other, and they're connected by an ancient bridge built in 1849, which was blown up in WWII but subsequently reconstructed. Outside of Budapest, we camp beside the Danube and our conversation turns into a reality check over wine and a jar of delicious, heated-up Hungarian goulash.

Peter starts: "This car will never make it to India. Hell, we're lucky if we make it to Istanbul. Even though I love you to death, we're so isolated now. I miss the interaction with other people."

"I agree," I say. "Let's sell this piece of junk."

Now our route runs along Lake Balaton, and we camp on a hill overlooking the lake near Tihany, where gypsy music wafts up, adding a bit of ambiance as we dine on our warmed-up jarred food.

The next morning, we start early, pass through Keszthely, then slowly drive the back roads to cross the Yugoslavian border.

Yugoslavia

We turn south toward the Adriatic Sea. Since 1945, Josip Tito, this country's charismatic leader, has followed his own independent road to socialism, or national communism, as it is sometimes referred to here. He's cobbled together six republics—Bosnia and Herzegovina, Croatia, Macedonia, Montenegro, Slovenia, and Serbia—and defied the Soviets and the West by remaining nonaligned in the middle of the Cold War.

> **Yugoslavia**
>
> Josip Broz Tito ruled the country from 1944 as prime minister and later as president until his death in 1980. Then, the seven republics reverted to being separate countries again. Bosnia and Herzegovina, Croatia, Kosovo, Macedonia, Montenegro, Serbia, and Slovenia.

Thumbs Out!

There is a higher standard of living here. There are more cars and trucks and no bicycles or horse-drawn wagons on the highway, which we'd seen often in Hungary. We pass by Delnice on our way to the coast of the Adriatic Sea. We camp near Rijeka, with a view of this city on the sea. We snake along the coast on a road that swerves back and forth along the water beside mountains that jut up, gray and barren, above the deep blue sea. We camp in Karlobag, a small Croatian fishing town.

Peter has been feeling that bugs are living in his hair, so he decides to shave his head. He starts in with his razor, but soon realizes it is not a one-day job. He settles on doing one small section a day. It takes five days to finish, but in the interim, he's walking around the seaside towns with an evolving hairstyle that goes from patchy to a kind of mohawk to, finally, bald.

Peter minus his hair.

Small, walled towns that rely on fishing and tourism are scattered along the coast. Mostly, we see Germans on the beaches. Camping is never a problem, and we can always find showers in the plentiful auto campgrounds. Some days, there are gale-like winds called the Bura. One of these powerful gusts blows a shirt of Peter's that's in the back seat right out the window, and it floats kite-like out toward the sea. After a few minutes, Peter says, "You know, that was my favorite shirt." After another minute, I ask the bereft Peter, "Why didn't you ever wear it, then?"

Europe

> **Dubrovnik, Yugoslavia**
>
> The city was added to the UNESCO list of World Heritage Sites in 1979 with a population of 40,000.

Everyone's favorite city here is Dubrovnik, on the southern coast of Dalmatia. It's a diminutive ancient city that was once an independent city-state located within sturdy medieval fortifications and overlooking the Adriatic. Walking around the car-free old town, we visit the noble Baroque buildings, museums, and galleries. The town center is compact and easy to navigate, its narrow streets filled with restaurants and small shops. We camp outside of Cavtat, about a 20-minute drive south of Dubrovnik.

We spend our final night on the coast of Yugoslavia in Budva, Montenegro's oldest coastal town and the most famous beach resort in the country. The Germans are here in spades, with their hefty, bronzed bodies stuffed into their Speedos.

Since we're not allowed to pass through Albania, we head inland through the mountains that have held us to the coast this last week. We wander through Titograd, then, driving on a gravel road, head up the 6,066-foot, steep Cakor Pass, which offers great views looking back toward the Adriatic coast. We drive northeast to Kosovo, then circle back south to the Greek border. The border is closed when we arrive. Several campers have already settled in, and we join them for the night.

As the sun slowly grants us light, we realize that Peter's pocket watch is no longer on the driver's front seat, where he left it before going to sleep; also missing are a few dollars' worth of Yugoslavian dinar and our flashlight. We search around the seats. For security, we sleep with our windows two-thirds closed. We surmise that during the night, a snake arm came into our car. We are creeped out by this invasion of our space. Then, we remind ourselves that we have lost little and it's the first time we've been robbed. The border opens at 5:00 a.m. We are first in line, and cross into Greece.

Greece

In the afternoon, we make it to Thessaloniki, Greece. We walk around the city center and find a wine store displaying barrels. The merchant lets us sample the famous chalky-tasting retsina red wine. We tour the Triumphal Arch, an ancient Roman monument, and finish at the White Tower, a Byzantine fortress, then head to a bookstore nearby where we find books about Greece in English. We pass some appealing food shops, peer in the windows, and eventually stop at one where we sample stuffed green peppers, stuffed tomatoes, and eggplant with meat and potatoes wrapped into a pie of sorts.

We drive the short distance to Pella, the ancient capital of Macedonia until the end of the fifth century BC. Excavations, started here in 1958, have revealed large, well-built houses with colonnaded courts and rooms with impressive mosaic floors made of natural pebbles that portray scenes of a lion hunt and of Dionysus riding a panther. Under the streets, terracotta pipes were laid to distribute fresh water. The French tourists, forever enthralled by the world's antiquities, are here by the busloads, so we know we're on the right trail.

We camp in a field outside of Pella. In the morning, we sit with our coffee and notes, discussing where we want to go. We decide on Volos, a small peninsula that we can visit on our way to Athens.

Europe

In Volos, we find vistas of the warm, blue, crystal-clear Aegean Sea. Scenic, winding, seaside roads connect old, whitewashed mountain villages. We spend the next three nights on Volos at glorious camping spots and visiting different beaches, first Mylopotamos, then Afissos and Agria. We pick up supplies in the little villages on our way. The farmers are constantly coming and going to their fields. They invariably greet us as they pass by our parked camper car. We are lucky to have a full moon this night and we watch the moon play with the skittering clouds before we sleep. The next morning a woman who passed us on her way home the previous night brings us pears.

After Volos, on our way to Athens, we visit Delphi. We labor over mountains, with Monsieur Variant complaining, but we have a good road with views of valleys dotted with clusters of whitewashed buildings, their windows and doors trimmed in robin's-egg blue.

The valley below Delphi is an ocean of silvery-green olive groves. There are lots of tourists here, and we tail a tour, eavesdropping on the guide's descriptions. We learn that the ancient Greeks considered Delphi the center of the world.

Again, mechanical issues force us to find the local VW shops. The well-meaning small-town mechanics seem overmatched. At one point, having given the mechanics four hours to work on the car, we return to find the motor has been removed. Sensing our consternation, the friendly shop owner reassures us of his mechanics' prowess and takes us to lunch while his team puts the car back together again. This establishes two frequently encountered occurrences here. First, the ever-futile attempts to make our junker roadworthy, and second, our introduction to the Greek hospitality that never ends. We pay the ten-dollar bill and groan ahead.

Thumbs Out!

Another constant is the daytime heat, but it's followed by cooler nights that make our camping comfortable. When there's no wind, we fight off the pesky mosquitos.

In Athens, we head straight to the main highlight—the Acropolis, a fifth-century BC citadel on a hill where the Parthenon, the former Athenian Temple, perches above the city. After our first day of exploration on foot, we return to the parking lot below the Parthenon where we've left our quasi-camper. We now see other real campers parked beside us, preparing for the night. Spending the night here seems like a good idea to us, too. We get acquainted with our neighbors. It seems that the friendly Greek ethos rubs off on us tourists as well.

Since Monsieur Variant has been so persistently temperamental and we are harkening back to our old hitchhiking ways, we start displaying a "For Sale" sign in the car window every time we park. We hold firmly to our selling price of $350, since even though the car is fickle, it gets us to all the glorious antiquities of Greece.

Again, we fall into a pattern, camping below the Parthenon, having Greek-style coffee somewhere different every morning, then wandering around the museums, antiquities, and many colorful backstreets of Athens. After we stop at our favorite street vendor for lunch, we head to the Hilton Hotel lobby to avoid the afternoon heat and go on to dinner somewhere. From the parking lot with the other campers, we watch the Parthenon light show each evening before going to sleep. All this in our neighborhood below the Parthenon.

Every day, our handsome sidewalk sandwich vendor serves up his creations—fresh sesame rolls piled high with various slices of cheese, bologna, and veggies. His mother, who seems to be on the lookout for a woman he can marry, assists

Europe

him at the cart. She vets me thoroughly, mostly by patting her hands all over me. Peter stands aside and delights in this audition. I shake my head, feigning sorrow, and point to Peter and my wedding ring.

After we poke around, we discover the Hilton has a large, shady pool area with showers. The security line of defense to enter the hotel's pool is a simple sign-in log at the entrance desk. We sign in, exchanging smiles with the attendant, as Mr. and Mrs. Mickey Mantle. We slip right through. The next day, we sign in as Mr. and Mrs. Bart Starr.

Each day, the pool grows more crowded, filling up with members of an affinity group for Americans and Canadians of Greek Heritage, who are convening here. It seems that their main reason for attending is to show off and rub shoulders with the newly rich and famous members of their organization, including Telly Savalas, the American movie star. The scuttlebutt is that US Vice President Spiro Agnew will also be attending the conference. There is a flock of ostentatiously parked Cadillacs, mostly convertibles, in front of the hotel that have been shipped to Greece from America to call attention to their owners' success. Just down the street, a "For Sale" sign sits in the front window of our little car. These visitors are definitely not in the market for our Variant, parked down the street with its ever-hopeful sign.

We leave Athens for a few days to explore the south, and camp near Chora. By chance, we wander into an ongoing excavation site. There's so much for archaeologists to uncover in Greece, and this site is being worked by a small team led by Carl W. Blegen, the American archaeologist who has become internationally famous for his role in discovering ancient Greek treasures.

Thumbs Out!

There are no crowds, so it's easy to meet and chat with him. He's very much an elder who epitomizes his profession. He has one arm, wears the obligatory khaki outfit with a safari hat, and holds a tiny shovel to delicately brush away dirt, bit by bit. He graciously puts up with our basic questions. He oversees several sites and has worked in this area since 1938. Here he has unearthed a trove of pottery, tablets, and utensils. He posits to us that this might be the Palace of Nestor, built in 1200 BC. He shares with us that he started excavating in 1932, uncovering the ruins of Troy. A weird fact that he surprises us with is that the Romans invented concrete.

Parked in the countryside for our overnights, we make dinner with something homemade out of a jar from a local shop and take in the day's last light. The peasants pass by on their way home from the fields. They sit sidesaddle on their donkeys and always smile and wave. Curious and nosy, they often stop. If they're carrying anything from their fields, they offer us a sample of what they've harvested—grapes, plums, melon, or veggies. We try to reciprocate by offering to share any food we have. Sometimes vagabonds pass by in their horse-drawn wagons. They, on the other hand, often ask us for food or money.

In Greece, older men and women usually dress in black and share the field chores. In pursuit of after-work relaxation, only the men twiddle their worry beads and sip red retsina wine in the open-air cafés. I suppose their wives are home toiling over the hot stove, because I'm almost always the only female in a café. The local patrons are invariably curious and generous. The recorded music we hear, even if played by teens, is always traditional. We never hear Western pop music, not even the Beatles.

Europe

We return for one last day in Athens. We camp below the Parthenon; eat lunch with the handsome sandwich man and his warmhearted mom, who holds my hand; and spend the afternoon at the Hilton pool—signing in as Gen. and Mrs. Charles de Gaulle—before topping off the day watching our last light show at the Parthenon.

We get a couple of inquiries about our hatchback, but after a cursory inspection and test drive, both parties disappear.

Finally, we are heading for Istanbul with a short diversion behind the Iron Curtain into Bulgaria and Romania. Our final stop is one last visit to the sandwich man and his mom, then we're off.

Bulgaria

We drive through the Bulgarian border on August 2nd. The formalities are surprisingly straightforward as we pass into this Communist country. We take a break in Simitli and stroll around the square. We wander into a local grocery store and are shocked by the meager food display. Just a few simple glass jars of carrots on one shelf, pears on the next, and beans on the bottom shelf.

In the next small town, we walk to the square and see a dancing wedding procession accompanied by flute and drum music. The bride's dress is covered with pinned-on lev, the local currency. We follow the revelers to a large restaurant,

> **Bulgaria**
> This country became a member of NATO in 2004 and the European Union in 2007.

where a table is already spread with dishes, and a wedding cake is set to the side. Later, the groom hands out a gift of a T-shirt and a towel to each man, and the bride hands out a slip and a towel to each woman.

We are taking full advantage of the communal system and camp wherever we like. Here in Simitli, we sleep under some shady trees near a park.

We arrive in Sofia, Bulgaria's capital and one of the oldest cities in Europe. The city center is surprisingly beautiful, home to St. Alexander Nevsky Cathedral, one of the largest Orthodox churches in Europe. The historic and well-preserved center is intact, untouched by the stark Russian architecture that surrounds it.

Monsieur Variant needs attention, so we find a VW garage. The bill is way too high. Overhearing our ensuing argument, a Bulgarian man who had lived in New Zealand comes to our aid. He tells us he hates the system here. The government controls everything. To have enough money to live, he and his wife must both work. The wages are the equivalent of fifty cents an hour. Just to buy a car, he would have to save for twelve years. Of course, he is not able to get our bill lowered.

Later in the afternoon, we find a large hotel, where I sit in the lobby to cool off and rest while Peter continues his walk around town. I fall asleep in my chair.

Someone shakes my arm, "Are you okay?" A man who looks and talks like an American is asking. He is with a Bulgarian woman who has long, thick, black hair. I'm a little dazed.

He tells me, "I need 250 dollars to get my passport back. My wife, she's Bulgarian, must be out of the country by 4:00 p.m. tomorrow or she will be put in a concentration camp."

Europe

He explains that he was in jail, but to get out, he had to agree to an arranged marriage to this Bulgarian woman, who was able to secure his release.

Looking to assure me, he shows me lots of documents, all in Bulgarian.

Road in Bulgaria

Just then, Peter walks into the hotel and finds me with all these Bulgarian documents. The man starts talking to him, flipping the subject to our car. He tells Peter his friend can drive with us to Romania, but he will have to give us a special mixture of oils to enhance our car's performance.

This is getting strange, so Peter puts a halt to it: "Well, this is a lot to think about. Please write your name down for me, and we'll see what we can do."

We walk to the nearby American Embassy and ask the man at the desk if he knows Eugene Weber. "Sure do, he's our most notorious local con man," the desk attendant tells us. "Once he walked in here, said he'd been poisoned, and fell on the floor. We drove him to the hospital, and when we got there, he immediately fled the scene."

From Sofia, we begin the two-day drive to Romania. The roads are terrible. Mostly cobblestone and, when paved, rough. As the days continue to heat up, so does our car. Outside a small village, we park under a tree to cool off the engine, hoping for a breeze. A few people start hanging around. An old woman brings a chair and her small spinning wheel on stilts to set up her yarn-spinning operation next to our car. Another lady brings us a small bucket of pears. A horse-drawn wagon comes past us, and one old man says in English, "A Bulgarian Ford."

We laugh, and everyone smiles. The man translates his joke, but they ask him, "What's a Ford?"

When our car cools, we carry on, and as the sun slips down, we find a beautiful view over a vineyard and set up our camp.

Romania

When we cross the border into Romania, a guard assiduously inspects us, making us take everything out of the car. We comply, but the guard can interpret our body language and low grumpy voices as we put all our accumulated stuff back in the car. The guard, seeing how pointless this is, apologizes.

We spend another day driving to Bucharest, the capital. There, the city's beautiful Byzantine buildings are in stark contrast to the new Russian concrete monstrosities that sit side-by-side near their ancient neighbors.

We park on a shady street near the market.

We go to the American Embassy and sit in the library reading newspapers and books to find out about the country. The librarian comes over and asks, "What interests you when you travel?"

"The culture, architecture, and history."

"Do you like old architecture or modern?"

"We prefer the old."

Europe

> **Romania**
>
> The country was under Communist rule and Nicolae Ceausescu until he was overthrown in 1989. It is now a member of NATO and the EU.

"Yes, well we all prefer the old to the modern that looks all the same. For the last twenty years, we have had no say about that." She pauses, changing the subject. "Be sure to see the Village Museum, just outside the city."

The Village Museum is a large, spread-out settlement dotted with reconstructed houses from different rural parts of the country, painted in the bright colors of their regions. They are not garish. They are simple and attractive. Many have thatched roofs and wood fences with gates. Some gates look delicate and almost oriental, while others are sturdy and remind us of gates we saw in Switzerland. Some chairs on the front porches are made of twisted tree branches. There are also two churches.

The next day, we arrive at the ferry to cross the Danube on our way to Mamaia on the Black Sea. The traffic lined up to board the boat inches along. Peter turns the car off, leaves it in neutral, and pushes it in the line to keep it cool. The people walking by smile and wave, munching on sunflower seeds picking them right off the flowers.

In Mamaia, a four-mile strip of land between a lake and the Black Sea, the beach facing the Black Sea is packed. There are hundreds of Eastern and Western Europeans floating in the soft waves.

Mamaia Beach

Thumbs Out!

This is the first crowded beach we've seen since the Adriatic. It's the first time we see so many Italian tourists. Apparently, the Romanian language and the Italian language are similar, and the two countries have had a connection since the 1800s, mostly based on this linguistic similarity. In Greece and Yugoslavia, there were plenty of people on the beaches, but not packed like sardines as they are here.

We find the campground full. We park on the front lawn, use the shower, wash our car, drink some wine, and change into our best clothes to visit the local casino. My orange frock and Peter's corduroy pants make their first appearance since we were on board the ship to Naples.

We walk up the beach, where there's a congregation of gray concrete high-rise hotels, all with laundry hanging out of the windows. Each hotel has an open-air restaurant with a different type of band: rock, jazz, or waltz. The people passing by gather to watch the dancers. The styles are current, and the dancing tourists like showing off their best dance moves.

The casino at the first hotel we come to opens at 7:00 p.m., but to our dismay, it costs a dollar per person to enter. We find another one, but it's a dive, so we return with a plan. We will buy one entry, Peter will go in, find the best bet, win, and come out to get me. I plant myself on the front steps to wait.

Inside, Peter discovers that the smallest amount of money he can change into chips is 50 lev. He only has 25 lev. He wanders around, watching the gambling. Then the cashier approaches him and says he'll make an exception and exchange the 25 lev. Peter gets eight chips, goes up to the roulette table, and watches the ball land on red, over and over. So he plunks all his chips down on black. They spin the wheel, and the ball has one last bounce from black to red.

He comes back out looking a bit chagrined, and I know immediately that we lost our stash of lev. We return to our car in front of the campground and go to bed.

The next day, having had enough of the crowded beach and the overrun facilities, we begin driving back south toward the Bulgarian border. We crawl along behind the local drivers, who follow the rules exactly. If a sign directs them to slow down to 30, they slam on their brakes and drive 30. The draconian enforcement of laws, even traffic laws, results in total order here—no crime and very regulated traffic. However, the traffic rules don't seem to cover stopping on the highway. Drivers just stop when they feel like it and don't pull off the road. We become attentive, law-abiding, and very slow drivers.

It takes us a day to get back to Bulgaria, where we camp outside Burgas. Our car is in charge, not us. We often wait for it to cool, and it's gobbling oil. We continue on the narrow, bumpy roads, usually behind a very slow driver, to the turnoff that heads south toward Turkey. We bump along through wooded hills to the border—a small, minor crossing outside of Malko. Just inside Turkey, we find a place to camp for the night.

Turkey

We wake up and start toward Istanbul, 150 miles away. Our car is falling apart, but our future travel plans, still up in the air, will soon be falling into place. Straight away, we round a corner in the first village we come to and encounter a group of 20 camels at a watering hole in the middle of town. We continue sputtering along in our clunker, doubting whether we can make it to Istanbul. Peter pulls over, opens the hood, starts tinkering, and asks me for my nail file. He removes a small part and files it down. He puts it back in the motor. Voilá, we are back on the road.

Reflecting on Peter's lack of mechanical aptitude, I ask, "How the hell did you know what to do?"

"I've spent months watching mechanics. The spark plugs are the most common, easy fix."

We arrive in Istanbul around noon, park on a small tree-lined street near the city center and heave a sigh of relief. Peter puts the "For Sale" sign back in the window. Then we investigate the neighborhood. Three hours later, we return to our car and two men are standing beside it. The older man takes the lead, telling us, in perfect English, that he's interested in buying our car. We have not been in Turkey long, but he has the dark hair and mustache we've already noticed are so prevalent on men here. He says he's from Baghdad and works in the Iraqi Consulate in Istanbul. While he test drives our car with Peter, the Iraqi flips the script and gives Peter a sales pitch for reasons to visit the Paris of the East, Baghdad.

I wait with the other younger man, who is around thirty, has thin, sandy hair, no mustache, and looks more like a Norwegian tourist than a Turk. His name is Nadir. He is Turkish and tells me he was known as Ned when he went to college in the US. We are parked in front of his brother's pump repair shop. Nadir is back in Istanbul in his first job. He isn't interested in our car but thought we might be American and, having lived in the States, wanted to meet us.

Peter returns with the diplomat from the Iraqi Consulate, who is also not interested in the car but has arranged with Peter an appointment with him at the consulate tomorrow at 10:00 a.m. I introduce Peter to Nadir, and we chat for a while. Peter mentions that we're going to the consulate tomorrow to

Asia

get visas for Iraq. Nadir offers to drive us there now, then back here, so we'll know how to make the trip to the consulate tomorrow. Nadir tells us he went to college at San Francisco State College for four years. He is soft-spoken and appears genuine, so we trust him, but with eyes open. As we drive, he points out landmarks and explains the collective taxi system, known as *dolmus*, which plies the main roads.

Nadir drops us back at our car. The first highlight we visit is the Grand Bazaar. We find the Turks friendly, and, like the Greeks, they are quick to invite us for a cup of tea. I buy a new pair of sneakers for three dollars, and a man nearby fixes Peter's sneakers, gluing the loose flapping sole back on, gratis.

We bump into a Kiwi, a New Zealander, who's just arrived after crossing overland from India. He is happy to sit and tell us all about his adventures and mentions the Pudding Shop, a nearby café where all the foreign travelers convene.

Curious to see this place for ourselves, we walk directly to the Pudding Shop. It's a large place with several rooms. As we enter the front of the shop, where an array of Turkish Delight candies are on display, we smell roasting meat. The restaurant, in the next room, is packed with prototypical young hippie travelers from all over the world: young men with long hair, scraggly beards, and a few dreadlocks, most of them wearing harem pants, and young women with long hair wearing long, tie-dyed skirts.

Unbeknownst to us, we are at the official starting point of the so-called Hippie Trail, which extends from Istanbul to Kathmandu, Nepal, where legal hashish beckons. Everyone is looking for the cheapest way to travel the 3,500-mile route, which passes through Turkey, Iran, Afghanistan, Pakistan, and India to reach Nepal. We stick out like sore thumbs with our collared shirts and Peter's clean-shaven head.

Thumbs Out!

The café has an oversized bulletin board loaded with notes from people who are looking for rides in different directions and selling travel supplies, backpacks, and old clothes. We add a note about our car perchance to find a buyer for it here.

An added benefit of the Pudding Shop, which we will return to almost daily during our stay in Istanbul, is the tasty Turkish food. We especially like an eggplant dish and vegetable and meat shish kebabs.

> **Istanbul, Turkey**
>
> The Pudding Shop still exists today.

Our first night in Istanbul, we sleep in our car, with scarves draped over the windows to give us a bit of privacy. It's stiflingly hot and we barely sleep. We move our car to the main road in the morning, leaving it there for the day with its "For Sale" sign in the window.

We spot an open-air café in nearby Taksim Square. We order our first Turkish coffee for one lira, the equivalent of seven cents. Served in a small cup, it's dark, sweet, and delicious, with dark grounds at the bottom. We try the homemade yogurt made from sheep's milk and savor it. This will become our morning ritual.

We go to the Iraqi Consulate to meet the engaging diplomat who test-drove our car yesterday. He never mentions our car. With his help, we fill out reams of paperwork to apply for our visas, leave our passports, and are instructed to send a telegram to an office in Baghdad today. We are instantly enthralled with the thought of traveling from Constantinople to Mesopotamia, the cradle of civilization.

Asia

We send the telegram from the post office in Taksim Square and head next to the Turkish Automobile Association, a local office for auto touring help. We learn that to sell our car to a Turk requires lots of red tape. It's best, we are told, to sell our car to another foreigner, drive to the closest border, Bulgaria, with the buyer, leave Turkey with the car papers that we entered the country with, and exchange the ownership papers in the no-man's-land between the borders. The buyer now has the papers for the car in his name, then we check back into Turkey without the car entered in our passports.

In Istanbul, there are innumerable historical highlights, so we squeeze in one or two a day alongside our bureaucratic chores. We park the car in front of the city's Bosphorus Hilton, built in 1955 as the most modern hotel in Turkey, and take a dolmus to visit Topkapi Palace, where sultans lived for over three centuries. Being the city at the crossroads between East and West and the capital of the Ottoman Empire, Istanbul was a strategic location for trade and accumulating wealth from both sides. At the palace, there are thousands of ornate porcelain plates and jewels from many far-flung locations.

At the end of the day, we return our car to our parking place in front of Nadir's brother's shop. Tonight, on our second evening in Istanbul, it is cool, and we sleep soundly.

Nadir comes by in the morning and invites us to stay with him at his new, unfurnished apartment a block away. We accept, taking our foam pad, sleeping bags, and duffel bag to his place. It's got one bedroom with a single bed. His clothes are still in suitcases, the living room is empty, and there's a bathroom with a shower, as well as a kitchen with a small table but no chairs. Fine with us. We aren't given a key, so we leave when Nadir goes to work and return when he tells us he'll be home.

Thumbs Out!

We find the American Consulate. We talk to a clerk about going to Iraq, and he says, "Good luck getting a visa." We also explain that we're trying to sell our car. The clerk tells us we should come back and request an official document stating that we've transferred ownership of our car to its new buyer, as a precaution against a snag at the border.

We also take our car to a couple of VW shops for inspections. Their estimates to set this piece of junk right almost exceed our selling price. We demur, hoping to find a buyer. We drop our asking price.

On our fourth day in Istanbul, we check in at the Iraqi Consulate and are told our visas may take a few more days. We visit Hagia Sophia, completed in 537 AD to serve as the bishop's seat of Constantinople during the Byzantine Empire. For almost 500 years, from 1453 to 1922, Hagia Sophia was a mosque, and now it is a museum. When the magnificent Hagia Sophia was built, it was the largest cathedral in the world. St. Peter's in Rome is bigger, but it was built almost a thousand years after Hagia Sophia.

Every day we check the bulletin board at the Pudding Shop and re-park our car on the main road. The next antiquity we visit is Süleymaniye Mosque, built in the mid-1500s. Connected to the mosque is a small museum that tells us how the mosque's intricate tiles were made. After visiting the mosque, we climb Beyazıt Tower, a tall stone tower near the campus of Istanbul University, for a panoramic view of the entire city: the European side, and the Asian side, across the narrow Bosphorus Strait. We have not ventured to the Asian side yet.

Back at our car that evening, we discover a note tucked under the windshield wiper, an inquiry from a Mexican traveler, asking us to meet him at our car tomorrow morning at 10:00. We move our car back to its nightly parking place and return to Nadir's to sleep.

We get up early and change the oil in our car. Peter decides to add some heavy oil, similar to STP, to hopefully improve its performance. We move our car back to where it was parked yesterday. It's a busy Saturday morning on this street. Studying everyone walking toward our car, I finally spot a slim, handsome young man with neat, thick, longish black hair. He's wearing black jeans, a clean blue shirt, and a black jean jacket—definitely not a hippie. He has a warm smile and, as he approaches, holds out his hand for Peter to shake: "Guillermo Teutli, from Mexico City."

Peter shakes his hand, "Peter and Sally Blommer from Milwaukee, Wisconsin. First things first, would you like to drive the car?"

Peter hands the keys to Guillermo and gets in the passenger seat. I wait for them to return from the test drive. Peter and Guillermo reach a price of $315. We need to wait until Monday to complete the required paperwork. We agree to meet Guillermo at 7:00 p.m. tonight. We want to keep him close so he doesn't get away—one in the hand. We're thrilled that we can sell the car, but worry that it won't pass muster in the end.

We meet Guillermo at our favorite café on Taksim Square, the same one where we've been having breakfast since we arrived in Istanbul, then go out to dinner. Our conversation flows. We talk about everything—soccer, our experiences in Mexico City and in South America. He's been traveling for two months and wants to use the car to get out of the main European cities. We plan to meet at 10:00 a.m. the next day. We become a threesome.

Thumbs Out!

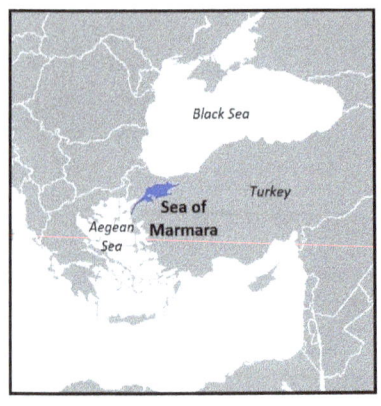

The next day, Sunday, Nadir invites us to drive along the Bosphorus Strait but says he doesn't have room for Guillermo. Peter finds Guillermo and makes a plan to meet him on Monday.

We join Nadir and drive north along the Bosphorus. The route is wooded and dotted with beautiful mansions. The strait itself is 20 miles long, a narrow corridor flowing between the Mediterranean and the Black Sea. It's a fish migration lane filled with colorful fishing boats. Then we cut back south to the Sea of Marmara, which connects to the Aegean Sea via the Dardanelles, another narrow strait. We swim at Florya Beach, on the outskirts of Istanbul, before returning to the city in the evening.

On Monday, we wake up early and go to clean up the car. We're both conflicted because we like the simpatico Guillermo and know the car is a piece of junk. We pick him up at his hotel, and he drives from there. First, we go to the American Consulate, where they make an official document that shows we sold the car to Guillermo. Next, Guillermo wants to change money. He goes to the bank, and we go back to Nadir's. We return to Guillermo, who now says he wants the sponge padding for the car. We're happy to throw it in.

Now, since Nadir has already left his apartment, and we have to await his return at the end of the day, we have time to spare. Guillermo says, "Then I have time to see the Grand Bazaar before I leave Istanbul."

Asia

At the crowded Bazaar, Peter thinks he spots a friend of ours from Milwaukee. She's very distinctive looking, tall, slender, with long, straight, blonde hair. Not being entirely sure, he walks up to her and says, "I know you."

She's surprised.

He repeats, "I know you."

I hear a familiar cackle and know instantly it's Weezie, my longtime friend who was in our wedding, now nine months ago. There are hugs all around. We introduce Guillermo to Weezie and her husband, Butch, and the five of us move on to a café to talk. Rapid-fire animated catch-up conversation ensues.

Peter says, "What are the chances we would meet in the Bazaar in Istanbul?"

Weezie says, "About a million to one."

We explain that we're on our way to the border to sell our car, and that we'll be back late, and we make a date to meet for breakfast tomorrow.

We leave our friends and go to Nadir's, pick up the sponge padding, and start for the border. Peter is driving ever so slowly, and we're all in high spirits. After twenty miles, the car stops dead, kaput. Peter suspects his last-ditch restorative effort with the STP is the problem but doesn't share this with Guillermo.

We hire a truck to transport us and our car back to Guillermo's preferred VW garage in Istanbul. The truck backs up into the ditch next to the car, and we push the car onto the flatbed. We all ride in the car on the flatbed. We're so relieved to still have Guillermo on the hook.

Arriving at the garage, the truck backs up to a ramp and we push the car onto it. The garage is closed, so we are all awaiting the mechanic's verdict in the morning. Guillermo

Thumbs Out!

sleeps in the car, and we return to Nadir's. That night, Nadir reads to us from the Turkish newspaper that there's a cholera outbreak, and everyone is advised to get shots.

In the morning, I go to meet Weezie and Butch. Peter goes to meet Guillermo at the garage. Soon, Peter and Guillermo join us. We all discuss the cholera outbreak and decide to get the immunizations.

I spend the day touring with Weezie and Butch. Butch drives their rental car to the Dolmabahçe Palace on the coast of the Bosphorus Strait. In the meantime, Peter and Guillermo are back at the VW garage to assess the damages. They're told it will take five days to make Monsieur Variant operational.

Our fivesome meets up for dinner around 7:00. We've all gotten our cholera shots at the local pharmacy. This is a goodbye dinner, since Weezie and Butch are flying back home in the morning. After dinner, we walk them back to their hotel.

As we stroll, Peter hearkens back to one of his favorite stories of Weezie and me in high school. Weezie was a top student and she, as usual, posted an "A" on a history exam we just finished. I stated my admiration for her scholarly prowess.

Her retort to me, "Yeah, but you get an "A" in life."

Now Peter adds, "Amen."

We go to Nadir's, and Guillermo goes back to his car, now his new residence, to sleep. After all, in effect, this car is his, since he's now paying for all the repairs.

We meet Guillermo in the morning and decide to take a camping trip together to the Princes' Islands, nine small islands in the Sea of Marmara, the largest of which is Büyükada. The trip to Büyükada is about fifteen miles by

Asia

ferry from Istanbul. Getting off the ferry, we're surprised to discover that there are no motorized vehicles in Büyükada, only horse-drawn carriages. There's one large pension with a restaurant that is close to the island's only small town, where there are a few cafés and stores. We find a campsite near the pension where there are other campers.

August 22nd is my dad's 72nd birthday, as he was born in 1898. We take the ferry back to Istanbul to call him. We put the call through at the post office in Taksim Square. After a two-hour wait, we have a weak connection. I have to shout into the phone at the top of my lungs: "Happy Birthday, Dad!"

Mom grabs the phone. "Where are you?"

"Istanbul."

"Where?"

I holler, "Turkey."

"Oh. Where to next?"

"India."

"Egypt?"

"No, In-di-a."

"Did you say India?"

"Yes."

The operator cuts in: "Time's up."

Silence. We're cut off before I can say love you and goodbye.

We go for Turkish coffee and yogurt and return to Büyükada on the ferry. In the dark, we walk back to our campsite. We pass the coffee shop in the pension where we've been having our morning coffee. The owner is just sitting down to eat. He asks us to join him and brings us beer, salads, and kebabs. He tells us that this was Leon Trotsky's home for a time after he was exiled from the Soviet Union from 1929 to 1933.

Thumbs Out!

We return to our campsite and find Guillermo. He's been busy all day meeting other campers. There's a breeze, and we all sleep well. With a new plan, planted in our heads at the Pudding Shop, to roughly follow the Hippie Trail east to India and, later, on to Kathmandu, Peter and I decide to go back to Istanbul a day early to get organized for the next part of our journey. Guillermo will camp one more night, then we'll meet him at the VW garage on Tuesday. We pay all our debts and share a carriage to the ferry with the pension's owner.

Back in Istanbul, we go to Nadir's brother's shop to pick up the keys to Nadir's apartment. He's decided that we can be trusted. We drop by the Iraqi Embassy and learn we've been denied visas. We go to the American Consulate library and read in the newspapers that there are huge street protests going on in Iraq. It's tit for tat, as the US is now also denying visas to the Iraqis.

We start reading about Iran. We return to Nadir's. He's at a wedding tonight. We now happily sleep on the floor. There are no mosquitos, and the floor is preferable to the ground.

On Tuesday morning, we meet Guillermo at the VW garage. We learn that the car will not be ready until 5:00 p.m., so we spend the next several hours revisiting the streets of Istanbul one last time with Guillermo until the car is ready.

In the evening, we set off for the border and finally make it there at 1:00 a.m. There's a long line of traffic, and Peter determines that we're allowed to bypass the line because we've had our cholera shots. I check my purse for our passports, but they're not there. Only now do we remember that the Iraqi Embassy did not return them when they told us we were denied visas. Mild-mannered, unflappable Guillermo turns the car around, gives the keys to Peter to drive, and gets in the passenger seat.

Asia

We arrive back at the VW garage around 5:00 a.m. We all get a few hours of sleep in our conveniently parked car. A knock on the window wakes us up. Guillermo sleepily tells the knocking mechanic that we're back for our suggested 300-mile checkup. It's been 12 nighttime hours since we picked the car up, so the garage guy gives us a quizzical look and shrugs.

Guillermo in his car.

The car is ready at 9:00 a.m., the 300-mile check-up completed in an hour. We drive to the Iraqi Embassy, pick up our passports, and begin driving back to the border.

There's some sort of road rally going on—sporty cars with numbers taped to their sides keep whizzing past us. A Citroën sedan with a sign declaring the car "Official" taped onto its side passes us at top speed. We see two laughing couples in the car. One of the men is driving, and someone in the back seat is waving a map in their hand. On this narrow, curvy, two-lane road, it strikes us as inordinately risky.

After 15 miles, we round a curve and see a truck blocking our lane up ahead. Then we spot the sedan that had passed us smashed under the truck. As we get close, we see the passengers who had been so gay now motionless after crashing into the truck, which must have pulled out suddenly onto the road.

We hear the sirens coming. We are slowly directed around the truck. We continue in stunned silence.

Thumbs Out!

Monsieur Variant jabs us one last time—the generator light goes on. We find yet another VW shop where they tweak something, and it's good to go. When we're presented with the bill, Peter overreacts, "This is way too much!"

The garage owner barks back, "You Americans do not own the world. Turkey is not American colony!"

Guillermo suggests that Peter step aside. Calm, cool Guillermo soothes the man and gets the price down for Mexico.

Since he's covered the latest batch of fixes, Guillermo pays Peter only $100 for the car. We hug and wish him good luck. We check back into Turkey with no car listed on Peter's passport. We take a bus to Istanbul and arrive at Nadir's at 11:15 p.m.

On Friday, August 28th, it's another sad goodbye as Nadir drives us to the bus station. We never fully understood his generosity, his showering us with friendship and kindness, expecting nothing in return. We've had good luck in 1970, but meeting Nadir was our best stroke of luck so far.

Since we've been denied entry into Iraq on our way to India, our new plan is to pass from eastern Turkey into Iran, then on to Afghanistan, before passing through western Pakistan to reach India. Today, on the first day of our car-less journey, we're leaving Istanbul in a comfortable new bus headed to Ankara, the capital of Turkey since 1923. But first our bus must board a ferry to cross the Bosphorus.

> **Bosphorus Bridge**
>
> Officially known as the 15th of July Martyrs' Bridge, it was the fourth-largest suspension bridge in the world upon its completion in 1973.

Asia

From the ferry, we can see pilings poking out of the water to support a bridge, now under construction, that will cross the Bosphorus and create the first true roadway connecting Europe and Asia.

On this six-hour bus ride taking us east into central Turkey, we initially pass through lush pine forests, then speed by rolling farmland. At prayer time, the bus stops, and the men exit, placing small rugs on the ground and, facing Mecca, kneel and bow their heads to the ground several times.

In Ankara, Turkey's second-largest city after Istanbul, we take a dolmus to the inexpensive hotel recommended by a Pudding Shop acquaintance. We see no other travelers here, so we suspect this is a place that people on the Hippie Trail just pass through. We walk through unimaginative concrete buildings in the city center, but then discover a beautiful park. It has an artificial lake and it's filled with tall trees and lined with restaurants. We dine on delicious kebabs at a restaurant facing the lake, then return to our hotel. Peter busies himself calculating how much we spent on Monsieur Variant per day: $8.83, all in.

At 4:00 a.m., we are awakened by the call to prayer, an amplified chant that emanates from all the mosques five times a day. We spend one more day in Ankara, visiting the old walled portion of this sprawling city, the Museum of Anatolian Civilizations, and the Ethnography Museum.

The next morning, while we're enjoying Turkish coffee at a café near our hotel, we hear army bands marching down the street. Today is a holiday called Victory Day, or Armed Forces Day. After the parade, we take a dolmus to the bus station, where we catch a bus for Erzurum, our last stop in Turkey, some 600 miles to the east.

Thumbs Out!

In addition to having dark hair and mustaches, almost all of the men in Turkey wear black suit coats and visored flat caps, or newsboy caps, as Peter calls them. The men often hold hands or arms while walking. The women we see are always fully covered. The farther east we travel into Turkey, the more fundamentalist it becomes and the more covered up the women become. In the streets and on the buses, we are met with cold stares, and interaction is almost impossible. This is an unwelcome and abrupt transition from Istanbul. I'm especially careful to dress respectfully, wearing long pants, a long-sleeved shirt, and a scarf, wrapped like a babushka over my blonde hair.

Our bus's brakes start to fail and we're delayed twice for repairs. Two English-speaking Turkish passengers from the bus approach us during these hour-long breaks, and after a while, the men begin to rant about their stifled life here. "Given enough money, I'd leave for Australia tomorrow with my family," one said.

Heading south now through pine forests, we climb over the steppes. We welcome stops in towns along the way and are happy to cross paths one morning with a couple we met back at the Pudding Shop who are riding a motorcycle on their way to India. The couple, however, sort of blows us off when some fellow hippies arrive. Peter, with his hair but a stubble, and me, with my standard functional travel uniform, don't resonate.

Also, for the first time in Turkey, we're encountering overt shunning from locals. This starkly contrasts with how Nadir, our former landlord in cosmopolitan Istanbul, treated us, and, in retrospect, makes us appreciate him all the more. He was the quintessential helpful stranger: kind, shy, circumspect, and sharing.

Asia

Contemplating Nadir's generosity prompts us to look back at how we've been received from the start of our journey. In Mexico, we were sometimes dismissed as gringos. Throughout Central and South America, we were held responsible for America's history of political interference. In Europe, we heard snarky remarks about Americans being noisy and boorish. However, we've mostly been unaffected by these stereotypical views due to our close-to-the-ground style of travel.

We finally arrive in Erzurum around 4:30 p.m. We pick out the usual cheap hotel and then wander around the earth-toned adobe town. We catch the mellow, earthy scent of the drying animal dung piles in front of the houses. This is used for fuel for their cooking fires and heat in the winter. Here, the women are covered in long dresses that are more colorful than the dresses we've seen women wear elsewhere in Turkey. The tea shops on every corner are filled only with men. We enjoy Adana kebabs, made of meat similar to hamburger, along with stewed onions, peppers, and fresh flatbread for dinner.

On Tuesday, we set off for the border with Iran at 6:30 a.m. The bus breaks down, but it's fixed in no time. We are dropped in a town close to the border but need to take a minivan the rest of the way.

The minivan meanders around, dropping off the other passengers until we are the only passengers left. The yin of this circuitous route is that we pass by a 38-foot-deep hole that was created by a meteor in 1920. The yang is the extended trip so close to the border. Finally, the driver grumpily drops us at the crossing point.

Thumbs Out!

Iran

While we wait for our passports to be reviewed and processed by the officials, we reunite with the motorcycle couple and another couple that we refer to as the Beard and the Blonde. After we cross the border, because of the spotty bus service, we decide to hitchhike the short distance to Maku. We find a hotel where the Beard and the Blonde have already checked in.

Things are strikingly different in Iran. The women wear Western clothes, with only a token head covering, and the men don't ogle me; they also give me my space as they walk past. The men hang out in tea shops smoking water pipes and sometimes even smiling at us. The friendly elderly hotel clerk walks us to the nearby bus station and helps us buy our bus tickets to Tabriz. He then escorts us back to our room, making sure the lamp that didn't work earlier has been fixed, but disregarding the bedsheets that haven't been changed. Before the clerk leaves us, he first kisses Peter on both cheeks, then me on both cheeks. Peter says, "The last man to kiss me on both cheeks was Papa."

Caravan of camels.

The next morning, we oversleep and rush to the bus, which fortunately hasn't left yet. Peter has time to run back to the hotel and pay.

Asia

Hustling back to the bus, he encounters a smiling policeman who says, "When you return, you must stay at my house."

"Why?"

"Because I love you."

Peter tells me his story and says, "Maybe here, the men are more interested in me."

The bus taking us toward Tehran passes through the treeless countryside, which is punctuated with more small villages made up of adobe houses with huge piles of dung drying beside them. Caravans of camels loaded with packs trudge single file beside the road. When we stop in the villages, there are always silver shops with intricate, handmade artifacts to entertain us.

But long, slow, hot bus rides like this, with only occasional points of interest, induce a kind of stupor. Peter, as always, is occupied overseeing the driver's progress. We are in our seats of choice in the front row on the door side of the bus. I'm next to the window, slumped in slumber. Suddenly, the bus stops and I slither out of my seat, pass under the handrail and end up crouched, collapsed like an accordion, in the stairwell. I pick myself up, walk up the stairs, and return to my seat unscathed. Peter tells me how graceful I was and scores it a ten.

We overnight in Tabriz, an oversized village on our route to Tehran. The next morning, back on the bus, we befriend an Armenian who lives in Tehran. He speaks English and tells us about living in an Armenian enclave in Tehran, where he has little contact with the Iranians. Everyone he knows is Armenian and a business owner, mostly running silver shops. Peter likens this to the Jewish diaspora. The Armenian agrees: "We, too, yearn for our own homeland."

Thumbs Out!

In Tehran, we spend a few hours finding a hotel and end up in a run-down hotel near the city center that's filled with travelers we've come to recognize. The Hippie Trail is thousands of miles long and an inch wide. Every day now, in buses, hotels, and restaurants, we encounter European long-haul travelers. Often we meet multiple times, always exchanging information that, in effect, keeps us tethered to the Hippie Trail. We spend three days in Tehran and are thankful that if an Iranian speaks another language, it's usually English. Even the written numerical symbols are different, so we make an effort to learn how to count from one to ten in Persian to help us with addresses, ticket numbers, seat numbers, and prices. But Farsi, the Persian language, is to us indecipherable, read right to left, in the artistic looping script that forms its alphabet. We prevail on English-speaking locals to write notes in Farsi that we can pass on to get our everyday needs met.

With no intention of making a purchase, we visit many different carpet shops, being curious to learn about the different styles and colors that distinguish the rugs from different areas of Iran. In the shops, we enjoy watching the carpet makers weave rugs on large looms.

Using our Farsi notes, we buy tickets for the bus to Mashhad, in eastern Iran. On Friday, September 4th, most shops and all offices are closed in Iran. The Pakistani Embassy, where we want to pick up visas, will reopen on Sunday. Unlike Turkey, which adheres to the Western weekend schedule, with official offices closed on Sunday, the weekend in Iran falls on Friday and Saturday.

Following a coup covertly supported by the United States and Great Britain, the Shah of Iran, Mohammad Reza Pahlavi, has been the widely reviled absolute monarch here

Asia

> **Mohammad Reza Pahlavi, the Shah of Iran**
>
> Fled the county in 1979, and Ayatollah Khomeini returned after 15 years of exile and took control.

since 1953. His oppressive but secular regime provides a veneer of modernity. SAVAK, the secret police, enforces the safety and the peace. But the occasional English-speaking Iranians we encounter almost always give away their intense dislike for their shah.

We see to our practical needs: collecting visas for Pakistan, malaria pills, intestinal relief meds, and a souvenir—a small, backward 1971 Persian calendar.

After leaving Tehran, our bus hugs the coast of the lush green Caspian Sea, then turns back south into the redundant dry landscape. Every time the bus pulls over for a break, we sit at a table in the bus restaurant and a waiter brings tea, flatbread, butter, and honey to each person at the table at no charge.

During this all-day ride, we have one encounter that begs the question, *What the hell?* Our slow-moving bus passes an even slower-moving, smoke-belching steam engine, chugging along the adjacent rail tracks at 15 mph. Seated next to us is an Iranian Air Force member, Safar Rooz, who was trained in the US. He tells us the train was built in England in 1920 and is now attempting the Sisyphean feat of circling the globe before being retired. He says the train left England six months ago. This feat seems rather far-fetched to us—*how does a train cross an ocean?* —but so far so good.

At the next rest stop, we have dinner with Safar, who clandestinely buys us our meal while we are keeping our eyes on the driver for a clue as to when we are leaving. It's late at

Thumbs Out!

night, it's a slow trip, and the bus finally makes a stop at a basic hotel that turns out to be already full. Most of the passengers simply leave the bus and lie on the ground for a few hours. I fall asleep in my bus seat, but then am poked awake. It is Junior, the young bus helper: "Mister, Mister."

"No, I'm Mrs."

"Mister, Mister." He points outside, which I interpret as him saying it's better out there. I shake my head no and go back to sleep.

Back on the road in the morning, every time we encounter any perceived road hazard, one of the older passengers shouts out a short prayer, then the other passengers reply in chorus with the equivalent of *Amen, may Allah be with you*, in Farsi.

It's only now that we learn Mashhad, our next stop, is considered the second most holy Muslim city after Mecca. Most Iranians can't afford the long trip to Mecca, so they opt for a mini Hajj to Mashhad, the second-largest city in Iran after Tehran. We see more and more camel caravans and nomad tent cities as the passengers chant their beautiful prayers in Farsi.

In minaret-dotted Mashhad, Safar helps us find a no-frills hotel where a few other long-haul Western travelers are staying. In the morning, Safar returns with two friends to guide us to the city museum where we, as apparent novelties, are the subject of many photos taken by the Iranian patrons. We visit the golden-domed mosques that by being fully aware of the restrictions of Islam, I cannot enter.

Like any good tour guide, Safar waits until the end of our tour to overwhelm us with the most holy Goharshad Mosque. It's huge, with a blue-tiled, onion-shaped dome, and filled with large crowds of the Muslim faithful. It's abundantly clear that I, a female infidel, cannot enter. Peter can enter in his long pants and shirt but decides to wait to enter later without Safar. One of Safar's friends leads us all to his house and feeds us royally with a delicious meal of ghormeh sabzi, the national dish of Iran—a stew of herbs, parsley, cilantro, chives, kidney beans, and lamb. This was served alongside a noodle, herb, and yogurt soup and followed by fruit and nuts for dessert. It seems that Iranians, Turks, and Greeks all borrow from each other culinarily. Then Safar takes us back to our hotel by cab and wishes us safe travels.

It seems that we're more accepted by the hippies as Peter's hair grows out. At the hotel, we again meet some of our hippie friends, including Archie, a Dutch guy we'd met earlier in Tehran, who accompanies us back to the Goharshad Mosque. Archie tells us that there's a place to rent a chador, and takes us there. I put one on. I'm covered from head to toe and looking out of the gauzy front.

I'm only allowed in the women's area, which is adjacent to and far smaller than the men's area. Peter enters the main area and I go into the one designated for women. I can enjoy a limited view of the delicately colored mosaic tiles and the curving Persian architecture, which includes a gold dome and a separate turquoise dome, as well as a room that I can peer into with stone carvings on the ceiling. It is magnificent. Back outside, I'm thinking I enjoy wearing this chador. It almost feels flirtatious, *I can see you, but you can't see me.* I approach Peter, now talking to an English-speaking Iranian, who, upon seeing me, bursts out laughing uncontrollably.

Peter asks him, "What's so funny?"

I peek out of the head covering and say, "Hello."

He says, "I can tell you are not Iranian because an Iranian woman takes care that the chador is even all the way around and walks slowly."

Peter laughs. "You are a rare Iranian with circumspect, soft religious views."

The man responds, "Yes, I am. Thank you."

Afghanistan

We catch an old bus filled with travelers, most of whom we know, to the Afghan border. After the long entry process, we collectively negotiate transport in another bus to Herat. The driver loads every inch of space with more and more travelers. We arrive very late, and after all the other passengers get off, the driver, using pantomime communication, invites us to sleep on the bus, which we do.

Unlike Mashhad, Herat is a popular layover on the Hippie Trail. In the morning, we choose the Super Beyzad Hotel, already full of European travelers, in the city center. Hashish is quasi-legal in Afghanistan and often offered to us by travelers and locals alike. The Afghans seldom smoke hash, but most of the hippies are stoned all day. Herat is not laid out on a grid—its streets meander through the adobe-style neighborhoods—so, paying attention to landmarks amid the subtle earth tones is essential.

The Afghan men are rugged and weathered-looking. They usually wear turbans and often have angular features and piercing dark eyes. All the women are completely covered in their long, black burqas, seeing through a screen over their eyes.

We are escaping the midday heat in the hotel. Peter wanders down the hall and is invited into a couple's room. Rebecca, an American girl, confesses that they lie on their bed every day from 1 o'clock to 3 o'clock and "worship the fan." Oh, yes, while smoking hash. Peter is curious and accepts the invitation to sample their primo stuff. The dope is potent, so just a few hits does Peter in. He returns to the room giggling and confessing the obvious to me. I suggest that he take a walk. He wanders around the streets of Herat for a couple of hours, agog. He gets lost but eventually returns. Then we go together and get some hash from the couple and come back to our room, smoke, and giggle together.

We are starting to meet travelers returning from Nepal who tell us about the Khyber Restaurant in Kabul. It's a beacon for the overlanders going in either direction. The only place to have burgers, fries, and milkshakes. The seed is planted for us to reconnect with this familiar food.

Until Herat, we've had little choice of transport or what route to take. Now, there are three different ways to get to Kabul in eastern Afghanistan that we can choose from. The first is to continue on the Hippie Trail through the south, riding on a bus on the American-made, paved highway that passes through Kandahar, and arrive in two days. The second is to pass through the rugged interior mountains of central Afghanistan. This route would offer no public transportation or even paved roads—just tracks, rudimentary infrastructure, and sometimes travel by donkey or camel. It would take up to a month to cover.

> **Herat, Afghanistan**
>
> Heret is the third-largest city in Afghanistan. In 1979, following the Soviet invasion, the USSR established a military command here. In 2020, it had a population of 575,000.

The third option, which we choose, is a once-a-week bus service that will take us along Afghanistan's northern border with the USSR, riding mostly on unpaved roads through the

Thumbs Out!

northern desert via Mazar-i-Sharif. The estimated time to Kabul is five to seven days. The appeal for us is to get off the main path of the Hippie Trail for a while and immerse ourselves in the country. I'm all in. Peter has some misgivings, but we commit and buy tickets.

On Saturday, we arrive at the pickup location and discover that the bus we'll ride is an old, yellow, American school bus with straight-backed seats. Our bus tickets have no seat numbers, so we want to board early. As we approach the bus, an older man comes up to Peter, taps his shoulder for attention, and starts unraveling bandages around his arm, to reveal a wound encrusted with dried blood. Other passengers line up behind the man. Peter shakes his head and says, "No doctor, no doctor." The man doesn't understand until the bus agent intervenes and explains to them that Peter is only a passenger on the bus and he isn't a doctor.

The bus leaves two hours late. Soon it feels like being in a high-rise elevator where someone has pressed the button for every floor. We stop for gas, prayers, food, a break, repairs, more prayers, and a punctured tire. And by the time we reach our first scheduled stop, in Qal`eh-ye at 1:00 a.m., we're already 24 hours behind schedule.

We haven't seen any other vehicles on this sand track. Without a clue of what other transportation we can pick up, we decide to get off the school bus, mostly because its seats, designed for eight-year-olds, are killing us. *No mas!* We want our money back, but the driver refuses. We need an arbitrator.

That night, we sleep with the other bus passengers on wooden plank beds outside of a full hotel. At first light, the driver wakes everybody up. We pile into the bus and drive a short distance to a one-story house, the regional chief's residence and office. In this fiefdom, he's the judge, lawmaker,

Asia

administrator, and head policeman rolled into one. We leave the passengers packed in the bus, broiling in the hot sun, and, with the driver, go downstairs to a basement room with open windows near the ceiling, through which we can eye the yellow bus.

We are directed to sit on red pillows on a thick oriental carpet. The four of us sit in a circle on the floor with an industrial-sized fan blowing the warm air around the room. A young boy comes in with a bowl, a small towel, and a teapot full of warm water. We watch the boy move around our small group starting with the chief, who holds his hands over the bowl. The boy pours water on them and gives him the towel to dry. We all follow suit using the same towel. Then the boy leaves and comes back with grapes and tea.

The curious chief speaks some English and has questions. "Where are you from in America?"

Peter does all the talking and keeps his answers perfunctory. "New York." (No one here has heard of Milwaukee or even Chicago; if we name those cities, it leads to long discussions.)

"How do you like Afghanistan? How do you like our town?"

"We like Afghanistan very much. Your town is beautiful."

The chief, now wearing his judge's hat, turns to the bus driver and speaks in Dari. We watch the serious bus driver answer his questions. We're asked if we would like more tea. The verdict is swift and just. The bus driver is to return half of our fare. We all accept, without question. We are dismissed. The bus driver quickly returns the equivalent of $1.50.

The money values and cost of living change from country to country as we go. We adapt and find ourselves in serious negotiations over mere pennies. Peter simply entertains himself with this basically meaningless pursuit.

Thumbs Out!

As we walk a short distance down the only road toward the edge of the town, the bus passes by, spraying us with a fine, white sandy road powder in its wake. We head into a lean-to tea shop primarily to get away from the curious children but also to get some shade and, we hope, spot a ride.

Peter says, "You know, sometimes you're a little too brave. You've never had to suffer the consequences of a bad decision."

I say, "I always think it'll work out. I see no reason to worry. What good does it do?"

Peter: "Easy to say, hard to do. I get what you're saying, but you have to be aware of what's happening around you."

"I am."

"Well, I'll grant you this: no one I know has your intuitive instincts about people."

The landscape is barren, with light tan sand dunes and a dirt track. We can see for miles in either direction. There's not one motorized vehicle in this town, so we have to wait for some kind of transport to pass through. We're sitting in a tea shop surveying the desert track, hoping for any form of transportation, including camel caravans. One takeaway we've learned from months on the road: the lighter the traffic, the greater the chance of a ride being offered.

After some hours as the sun reaches its zenith, a smoke signal of stirred-up fine desert dust puts us on alert twenty minutes before the arrival of our first potential ride, a yellow Land Rover. We step out of the tea shop and make ourselves visible, waving our arms as they approach. The concept of hitchhiking here is totally unknown. They stop.

The four young men in the Land Rover make room for us in the way back. We crawl in and lean against the back of the rear seat, looking backward, legs outstretched on rugs next to a heap of surveying equipment shoved to one side. Three of the men are surveyors scouting a possible new road; the fourth is their driver. One of the surveyors speaks a little English. They understand we are Americans on our way to Mazar-i-Sharif. They are not going that far, but they can take us for a few days to about halfway. The accommodating English speaker says, "If you want to stop for photos or anything, just let us know."

The rutted route skirts around low sand dunes. Riding in the back, the sand road makes for a smooth, albeit slow, ride. Later in the afternoon, I ask to stop so I can pee. They park in the middle of the road. To find privacy, I trudge up a sand dune to the other side, out of sight. Later, Peter tells me that then all the men relieved themselves when I was out of view. As I return, I see that two of the Rovers have pulled out rugs and are kneeling to pray.

When they finish praying, I ask if I may take a photo of the men standing in front of the Land Rover. They comply. We carry on, and as the light in the sky dims, we arrive in a small village. The Rovers take us to the hotel where they plan to spend the night. The hotel is a big, older house made of adobe. The thick walls keep the daytime heat out. We can't check in because there's a banquet being held in the hall on the first floor. Cloths are spread out on the floor, and men are seated on pillows or on the floor along the walls. It's lit by kerosene lanterns in the middle, with full bowls of meat, vegetables, fruit, candies, and nuts amongst the lights. Barefoot boy servants walk around the food and lamps, filling cups with water.

We leave our bag at the front desk and walk with the Rovers a short distance to another adobe building lit by oil lamps and candles. We enter what looks like a small theatre

Thumbs Out!

without a stage. On one side, the adobe is formed into three-foot-tall steps with four tiers. There are small stairs against the wall to climb up. Lit candles flicker on levels one and three. We are the first in, and we all sit side by side on the first step between the lit candles. Others arrive and take seats higher up. Including the six of us, there are maybe a dozen people in the restaurant.

I am the only female. The kitchen is outside somewhere. A boy comes in with a bowl, a small towel, and a teapot. By now, Peter and I know this routine, and we all wash our hands. The same man who seated us brings in bowls on a tray. We're all served warm flatbread and a bowl of stew. There are no spoons, forks, knives, or napkins. We watch the Rovers to follow their lead. They slurp the broth, tipping the bowl to their mouths, dunk the bread in the broth then hold the bowl in their laps, picking out the meat and veggies with their left hands. Everyone talks in hushed tones while the candles create flickering, dreamlike shadows on the walls.

We return to the hotel, where no evidence of a banquet exists. We're issued an oil lamp and led through a garden behind the hotel, dense with bushes and small trees with a thin stream running through it. Men go to the left, there is a small plank bridge, and women go to the right of the stream, so these full-service facilities have running water. After Peter and I reconnect, we are shown to our room on the second floor with a neat, comfortable bed, two chairs, and an empty fireplace. There are no windows or electricity, and, of course, there's no bathroom.

The next morning, the Rovers invite us to continue on with them. The route now climbs up and down small sandy hills, and there are mountains in the distance. We climb up a low pass, then, in the distance ahead of us, see a tent the size

Asia

of two football fields surrounded by patches of green. As we get closer, we see herds of sheep and donkeys and a quota of camels. Next, we see women in colorful hijabs with trinkets that look like old coins dangling across their foreheads, plus lots of children playing near the tents. The men wear turbans and have rifles slung over their shoulders. We catch a glimpse into the enormous tent. The ceiling is comprised of hundreds of blankets patched together, and there are oil lamps glowing everywhere inside. There is a common space with pillows and lavish rugs surrounded by hanging cloth curtain walls, that looks like a city of rooms. These nomads live a good life with their green gardens, livestock, and enormous tent.

    Passing through different fiefdoms, each like its own small city, we stop occasionally for food or a break. In lieu of drinking well water, we mostly keep ourselves hydrated by eating the ever-present sweet, juicy melons. Again, Peter is assumed to be a doctor and is approached by an Afghan who

The Rovers

Thumbs Out!

Small nomad camp.

unwraps his injuries. A Rover explains that Peter is but a tourist.

Each fiefdom we pass through has its own omnipotent chief. We see a few women in the fiefdom towns who are fully covered in black clothing, indicating the deeper religiosity here, unlike the more colorfully dressed women nomads, and almost all the men are armed with old rifles. Nomads surround every oasis in the bone-dry desert. No vegetation grows on the undulating sand hills, behind which, to the north, lies the unmarked, unguarded border with the USSR. At one oasis, a blindfolded camel is turning a grinding mill—forever walking in circles. It's a tough neighborhood, but we feel safe. There is never any strife or confrontation. We make sure that we always appear respectful of their religion and way of life. Throughout history, Afghanistan has never been conquered or colonized. The rugged, unforgiving terrain and people remain indomitable.

Asia

For two days, we ride with the Rovers before they drop us off in a small town that is still a three-day drive away from Mazar-i-Sharif. We feel fortunate to have gotten this far, so we're content to chill, take in the crowded village market, and also keep an eye out for our next potential ride. A shop owner alerts us that another foreign shopper is in the market. We become like bees to honey, and it's not hard to spot the blond-haired traveler in a crowd of shrouded women and turbaned men.

When we stop and introduce ourselves, we act surprised, as if we've just happened upon him. The man, Siegfried, is German, and works with a non-governmental organization, or NGO. He's traveling with two other German NGO friends, plus an Afghan driver, in a Land Rover headed in the same direction we are. Siegfried listens to our proposal of joining them as far as the next town but feels he must run the idea past his travel companions. He thinks he's leaving us to find his friends outside the market. But we're determined to present our case in the best possible light, so we're hot on his heels.

"Necessity is the mother of invention" is another key lesson we've learned on the road. And by this time, we've honed our sales skills so well that we quickly land an invitation to ride with the Germans and their driver to the next town. Again, we find ourselves riding in the Land Rover's rear compartment, facing backward, traveling along the soft, dusty sand track. More mountains appear in the distance as we continue through the treeless sand hills. Nomad villages surround every oasis. The camel caravans moving between the villages are now longer and more frequent, with the last camel in each line wearing a big bell that rings with low rhythmic dongs. Ours is the only car on the road, so the

Thumbs Out!

camels and other animals become nervous and skittish as we pass.

In each village we pass through, the NGO men look to deposit us at a bus station. But there are none to be found, so, out of pity or kindness, they continue to keep us along for the ride. Late in the day, the men stop at an adobe hotel in Quaizar. We check into the hotel, but they put up their tent behind the hotel. We loan them our sleeping bags. We eat dinner together and are served oily rice and raisins, a dish we've become all too familiar with in recent days.

The next morning, we shove off, and the NGO men make a job-related stop in a village where they visit a small school. Sitting in on a class of six- to eight-year-old boys and girls, we notice that the teachers are playing games using dice or puzzles with English words on them to hold the kids' attention. Our traveling companions supply the teachers with some chalk for the blackboard, a few picture books, plus paper and pencils. Dari, derived from Persian, is the local language, but it's pointed out to us that the local elites speak Pashto.

Further along, we stop in Maimana for a lunch of melon and, again, our companions look for other transportation for us. There's none to be found. In the evening, we arrive in a tiny village with no discernible name but with a basic hotel, and here the NGOs also get a room. The hotel offers two hours of generator-supplied electricity from 7:00 to 9:00 p.m. We all go to dinner at a small café near the hotel and eat rice and raisins for the fourth night in a row.

The next day, in Sheberghan, we find a jeep transport station, and our saviors drop us off there. We buy our tickets for Mazar-i-Sharif and climb into the front seat of a large four-wheel-drive jeep retrofitted for public transportation and sit facing forward for the first time in five days. Initially, the track is still soft and rough but slowly, it smooths out as we go.

At a stop in a village, the driver approaches us and tries to shake us down for more money. We need another arbitrator. We find the omnipotent chief of the village fiefdom by asking for the Police. This negotiation is over in a minute—no grapes, no tea, no chitchat. He declares, "The tourist is right," and off we go. Peter forms a new theory: when there's a dispute, whoever calls "Police" first, wins.

The track becomes an asphalt road, and our driver and another jeep driver start racing, trying to overtake each other. It seems risky on this narrow, curvy road, so we resort to calling out "Police!" and our new theory holds true: the driver slows down and settles for second place.

In Mazar-i-Sharif, we reward ourselves for making it here and check into the best hotel we've stayed in since Iran, a room that will cost us 55 cents per night. But it's still rice and raisins for dinner.

We laboriously wash all our sand-encrusted belongings; it takes the entire morning. We buy bus tickets for Kabul and walk around the small city, visiting its grandiose, blue-tiled mosque, which has a curiously unusual cacophony of colors inside. I know now to rent a chador so I can enter to see it too.

At checkout, our hotel manager gives us a discount on our fifty-five-cent room as a kind gesture for staying two nights. We take a horse cart to the bus station, where we learn the bus is leaving an hour late. Finally, we depart and climb into the Hindu Kush Mountain range and over the Salang Pass, where we slow down to enter the highest road tunnel in the world. It's narrow, dark, and over a mile and a half long. It was built by the Soviets from 1958 to 1964, and it shortened this trip from three days to one.

Thumbs Out!

Coming out the Kabul side of the tunnel, we're greeted by a broad, panoramic vista of the road descending toward Kabul. The bus isn't comfortable, but it is fast. During one pit stop, an Afghan University student chats with us and shares his sad disdain for his backward country. We suggest that he could celebrate the simplicity of his life, his honorable fellow countrymen, and the majesty of his surroundings.

After arriving in Kabul, we check into the Nuristan Hotel and, from there, head directly to the Khyber Restaurant in Pashtunistan Square, a bustling area in the heart of the city. We are officially back on the Hippie Trail. The famous Khyber Restaurant turns out to be a cafeteria that offers institutionalized Western food, and it's packed with travelers. But the food is delicious. We dive in, slurping up milkshakes, burgers, and fries, then waddle back to our hotel, stuffed.

Over the next few days, we take care of business: securing visas to enter India, exploring various transportation options, gathering travel information from other overlanders, and are told where to obtain fake student IDs that we can use for discounts in India.

It's lunch and dinner every day at the Khyber. On our second day in Kabul, curiosity pulls us into a small local food store that is generously referred to as a supermarket. Peter is in a different aisle when he hears me say, "Hello, Donna."

And someone say back, "Hello, Sally."

It's another high school classmate of mine from Milwaukee. Donna and her husband John are in the Peace Corps. We find some seats in a tea shop for a long and wide-ranging talk. They live in a small village far from Kabul and only come to town once every two months. They confess that they're stoned every day, all day. We leave it at that, wishing them well.

Asia

That night at the Khyber Restaurant, we extrapolate the odds of meeting two of my 50 high school classmates on one pass through Asia. First Weezie in Istanbul, then Donna in Kabul. We figure it's many millions to one. Back at our hotel, in honor of our last night in Afghanistan, we smoke some hash ourselves. This potent hit takes us on a giggle trip, followed by a deep, peaceful sleep.

On Monday, September 21st, we board the bus to Peshawar, Pakistan, which will make one final stop in Afghanistan, in the city of Jalalabad—the bus labors up the dry western side of the Khyber Pass. Throughout history, these mountains have held back all invaders, including the covetous English colonizers. Early on, a few, including Alexander the Great and Marco Polo, crossed here, only passing through on their way to India. But in 1970, we are now approaching West Pakistan, as it's been known since the partition of India in 1947. Signs have instructed us not to take photos, inviting Peter to snap a stealth shot just before we arrive at customs on the Afghan side of the border. Passing through customs out of Afghanistan and into Western Pakistan is surprisingly easy.

Pakistan

We reach the crest of the pass and begin to descend through a tribal area, a no-man's land bristling with guns and still not under any kind of central government control. Fortunately, lingering intertribal hostilities are currently at a standstill. We've been told that this road is the most accident-prone in all of Asia. We hold on tight. The rocky hillsides sparkle because of the lead in them. We pass fortified villages and a few government watch stations and, as we descend on this narrow, paved, two-lane road with many

Thumbs Out!

sharp curves, we note the large, sacrosanct Ali Masjid Mosque, which no one in these parts would ever risk damaging.

From the border, it's only an hour to Peshawar. After we arrive in the city, we take a *tonga*, a horse-drawn, two-wheel carriage, to our hotel in the city's central circle. We have a delicious spicy chicken curry for dinner.

We stay one more night here because I wake up feeling punk and spend the day resting in bed. Meanwhile, Peter wanders around, being assaulted by the chaotic, colorful street life. Again, we have curry for dinner, our favorite food in the world, and maybe that's why I begin to feel better.

On Wednesday, we take a tonga to the Old Town and end up spending most of our day hanging out with a couple who are heading home to Cleveland after their two-year stint in the Peace Corps in Peshawar. They fill us in on current local politics. The big issue is the upcoming election in December. We are told that the vote will be completely regional, since the only commonality between the more powerful West Pakistan and the more populated East Pakistan is the Muslim religion.

Geographically, West and East Pakistan are separated by a thousand miles of India. Some think that the polarized results could lead to Pakistan splitting into two separate countries. The most popular West Pakistani politician, Ali Bhutto, addressing both parts of Pakistan in his speeches, has declared, "We rule here, you rule there."

The next day, we take a minibus to Rawalpindi, arriving in the early afternoon. From there, we take a tonga to nearby Islamabad. This newly built but already dirty, modern, utilitarian city leaves us uninspired, and after a short walkabout, we return to Rawalpindi.

Asia

After one night, we head to the minibus that will take us to Lahore. On our way to the bus, we encounter a lady walking with a snake draped around her neck. In Lahore, we find a typical hippie hotel, then walk to a complex known as the Mall, where we have a great Chinese meal at the Cathay Restaurant and enjoy another long talk about politics with the owner's son.

We lay over for a day in Lahore, take time to walk through the old walled city in the center of town and visit the iconic Badshahi Mosque, with its exterior of carved red sandstone and inlaid marble. From there, we board a double-decker bus to get to the famous Shalimar Gardens, which closes just as we arrive. We can only peek through the fence to take in some of the gardens' vastness and beauty. We return to the Cathay Restaurant in the Mall for dinner. Picking out restaurants has always been a crapshoot, so when we're served one good meal, we generally try to return the next day for, hopefully, a second good meal.

> **Pakistan**
>
> Until 1971, Pakistan consisted of two regions, East Pakistan and West Pakistan. In response to grave internal political problems that erupted in civil war in 1971, East Pakistan was proclaimed the independent country of Bangladesh.

India

At 7:00 a.m., we board a bus to the Indian frontier and arrive there four hours later. After we cross the border, it's another four miles to the closest town in India, that has a

Thumbs Out!

railroad station. The colonial English laid rail tracks throughout the whole of India that still offers us the best way to get around. The only available transportation to the rail station is a rickshaw, a two-seat extension behind a human-powered bicycle. We feel empathy for the skinny driver as we slowly roll, like the anachronistic colonizers of old, into town. The driver labors along, sweating in the midday heat, pulling his full load for mere pennies. We decide this is bad karma and resolve to avoid this condescending transport mode in the future. We are dropped off at the train station.

The train for Delhi leaves at 9:00 p.m., so we have time to tour this small rail hub town, but soon retreat from the sweltering heat and hang out in the train station's air-conditioned waiting room. On the overnight train, we sleep fitfully and uncomfortably, finally arriving in Delhi at 5:00 the next morning.

It's Sunday and we've finally made it to another of our pivotal, planned destinations. We check into a cheap and convenient "retiring room" in the railroad station; it's a large, clean room with a shower and toilet, a big upgrade for us.

In addition to daily entries in my diary, I have also kept a separate accounting of our daily living expenses since we left Milwaukee in January. Through Central Asia, these expenses have been but a couple dollars a day, just like in Central and South America. By living in our car and staying with friends in expensive Europe, we shaved our living expenses to only gas and food. Peter does the math after we get back to Milwaukee, and the all-in cost of our one-year world tour was $4,200. That's $2,100 per person or $6 per day per person. Included are airfares in Guatemala, Panama to Columbia, and finally from Nepal to Milwaukee. We took a cruise ship from Rio to Naples, Italy. We bought a car for a trip through

Asia

Europe to Turkey. The dollar is king, and we use the black market wherever possible. This sometimes gave us three or four times the bang for the buck.

For months, we've been warned by travelers returning from India to prepare ourselves for the cultural overload of everyday life. We've been able to spot these seasoned travelers on their way back west toward Europe by their loose-fitting clothing and oversized belts with additional holes punched in to help keep their pants up. It's a reminder to us to be aware of the tasty but dicey local food and water.

After settling in, we step out of our quiet, comfortable room into downtown New Delhi and immediately feel the body slam, confusion, and TKO of India. Horns honking; a cacophony of languages; smells of urine, incense, and spices; cows wandering aimlessly amongst the traffic. Men wearing only loincloths, with their chests and faces painted; women clad in brightly colored saris; Muslims in hijabs; plus a few men in crisp business attire.

We feel as if this vibrant, colorful, crowded, dirty, odoriferous, hot, foreign scene is kaleidoscoping around us. We wander the streets, just taking in our urban surroundings: a gridlock of rickshaws, pushcarts, donkey-drawn wagons, buses, cars and trucks, street vendors, and beggars looking for baksheesh. Numerous garish Hindu temples are adorned by statues of multi-armed deities, that bear oversized eyeballs, snakes, and lions; one is populated with petulant resident monkeys. Our eyes hurt, our heads spin, but for everyone around us, it's simply another ordinary day.

After a few hours, we take a crowded bus to Connaught Place, the central commercial street lined with formal colonial columned buildings. Most places are closed on Sunday except for the Indian Coffee House—aka ICH—a landmark restau-

Thumbs Out!

rant that is another well-known travelers' meeting place. Here we meet Helmut, a smart, good-natured Israeli traveler, with his friend James, a big, husky Australian. We trade travel stories for hours, and then, in the midafternoon, the four of us walk to the India Gate, a landmark arch that looks like the Arc de Triomphe in Paris.

We find an empty park and spontaneously sit on the shaded green grass to savor the peace and quiet. Two Indian boys, each carrying a basket, plop down on the lawn in front of us. One of them pulls out a flute and starts playing while the second uncovers one of the baskets. The flute entices a cobra to uncoil and rise out of one basket, while a mongoose pokes his nose out of the other. When we are eye to eye with the cobra, Peter, keeping his eyes locked with the cobra's, asks, "How much?"

The answer: "As you like."

The boys pass a baksheesh bowl to James, and all three men pay for the show voluntarily, albeit with a feeling of being under some duress, given their wish to avoid snakebites. Satisfied with their takeaway, the boys briskly cover the cobra and disappear with their baskets. We heave a sigh of relief and make a mental note to avoid covered baskets.

Snake charmers in New Delhi near the India Gate.

Asia

We decide to go to an early dinner, and being fully cognizant of the local health hazards, we continue to follow our old guidelines, looking for the busiest local food shop and avoiding the upscale tourist traps. We espy a thali restaurant, packed with locals sitting in a sea of tables. There's always a brightly lit clean thali restaurant in any town of size. There's no menu, and the vegetarian food is cheap, mass-produced, and made fresh daily. The main course is invariably lentils. We are guided to our own small table. A server places an empty metal compartmentalized tray in front of each of us, along with a spoon and a small plate of papadum crispy bread.

Then other servers, each carrying a shiny, two-quart bucket, ladle the contents of their buckets into our trays—first rice, then lentil stew, vegetables, and chutney, all delivered into the designated compartments. After dinner, we are served a sweet pudding made of rice and coconut milk, presented in a small metal dish along with a small spoon. Everything is delicious and quick. Luckily, we have eaten early because they serve only until the food runs out. They're closing as we leave. Our self-imposed dining rules have always served us well, even in India.

On Monday morning, we go to the Nepalese Embassy, where we run into the three German NGO workers who gave us a ride in their Land Rover for a few days in Northern Afghanistan. We are all speechless in surprise.

I say, "Did you know we refer to you three as our saviors?"

Peter chimes in, "Thanks again."

They've finished their NGO jobs and are traveling before returning to Germany.

We meet Helmut at the ICH for coffee, then walk around, soaking in the street life while we carry on with another wide-ranging conversation. An amiable 20-year-old Indian boy slowly blends in with us by casually pointing out points of interest. He's clever and compelling, and after a while, he gets to his ulterior motive: he is looking for sponsorship to emigrate to America. KK, the abbreviation of his unpronounceable name, is very persuasive, and we at least hear him out as he accompanies us on the one-hour walk back to our room at the railroad station. We have been snookered into betraying one of our core beliefs: If they approach you, don't trust them. If you approach them, you can trust them.

On Tuesday, we meet Helmut at the ICH again and walk to the American Embassy to check out the sponsorship process. As we suspected, it's not simple or quick. Helmut takes us to eat at the nearby Cellar Restaurant, another Westernized establishment with burgers and rock music. Outside the restaurant, by design, we meet up with KK, informing him that we can't help him since we're leaving tomorrow. KK gives us the frequently used Indian head wobble, a tiny, side-to-side, circular head movement, like the movement of a bobblehead, which we have come to interpret as meaning neither yes nor no, but as an indication of no commitment. It can also convey I understand, it's OK, or maybe. I want to grab his head in my two hands and turn it left to right for no, then up and down for yes, and ask, "Which one do you mean?" But I realize that his wobble, in this case, means "I understand."

Nevertheless, KK continues with us as our de facto guide. He shows us a Sikh temple. The Sikh men are recognizable by their neatly tied turbans, which conceal their uncut hair tied in a bun; their beards; and the long, loose, white tunics they wear over baggy trousers. Almost all of them have the last name of Singh. They were known for their integrity while they served with distinction in the former English colonial army,

Asia

and they're now often appointed to serve as incorruptible policemen. KK suggests that if we have trouble, we should find a Sikh, since it's part of their religious beliefs to help travelers.

KK educates us about the intricacies of the caste system, pointing out the "untouchables," living on the streets as the lowest stratum of the caste system. Even the revered pacifist leader Mahatma Gandhi didn't openly question the caste system, KK explains.

Later, alone with Peter, I confess my feelings of utter hopelessness for India. How did the British ever think they could rule this place? Since 1950, the Indian people have been attempting to rule this jumble as an independent democratic republic.

When our railroad room is no longer available, we buy third-class train tickets to Agra for the sole purpose of seeing the Taj Mahal. Our train is scheduled to leave at 8:00 p.m. tonight. In India, the train system offers a myriad of classes. There's first-class, air-conditioned with padded seats; second-class, no air-conditioning with designated hard seats; and third-class, very cheap, no assigned seats, and always overbooked. There are also two classes of sleeper cars for overnight trips, one with soft beds and another cheaper one with harder beds.

The loose oversight on the train allows us to escape the crowded third-class coach compartment, where there are no available seats, and slip into second-class to commandeer two leftover hard seats. Our ploy is, if caught, to just act confused and, of course, offer to comply with the rules. Usually, we get away with such ploys by feigning ignorance.

After arriving in Agra at 10:45 p.m., we share a cab with three other travelers to the government-run tourist bunga-

Thumbs Out!

lows, which are fully booked. We're so tired that we sleep on couches in the waiting room adjacent to the reception area, and they allow us to use the bathrooms.

Waking up in Agra on Wednesday, we inquire and find there are no rooms available for the night. We leave our bag at the bungalows and take a rickshaw to the Taj. There is just no getting around taking these human-powered bicycle rickshaws. They are plentiful, cheap, and convenient.

We are dropped off at noon at the elegant red sandstone gate to the Taj Mahal, and the driver, whom we call Ricky, agrees to pick us up at the Red Fort, a mile away, later in the afternoon.

The Taj Mahal (public domain)

Taj Mahal

In 2025, over 7 million visitors, including 800,000 foreigners, will visit the Taj. It is closed on Fridays and you can purchase tickets online.

Asia

The Taj Mahal was built in the 17th century by Mughal Emperor Shah Jahan as a mausoleum in memory of his deceased wife and beloved companion, Mumtaz Mahal. A love story. The beauty of the Taj is awe-inspiring. We wander inside the main building, which is decorated with swirling Arabic calligraphy inlaid with semiprecious jewels, including lapis lazuli, jade, crystal, and turquoise. It's a large space with fake coffins in the middle. We spend hours outside, ogling the majesty from different vantage points. There are four identical simple, elegant facades, with one facing a reflection pool, where we spend most of our time. The ivory-colored marble takes on different hues as the blue sky clouds over and the sun changes angles. Not only are we viewing one of the most magnificent edifices in the world, but we're in an island of tranquility. It is simply open to anyone, with no entry fee, but it's not crowded.

We walk the mile to visit the Red Fort, an old royal palace. It's a square mile of red sandstone walls surrounding a palace, mosque, and numerous outbuildings. The best part is the view from here of the Taj Mahal, now bathed in pink with the setting sun. The Mughal Empire was at its height when the Taj Mahal was built. Today, we look back at the so-called advanced civilizations that grew and then disappeared, and we wonder how history will view the empires of today.

We find Ricky sleeping in his passenger seat, and he takes us back to the bungalows. We have a curry dinner nearby and board our next train, obtaining a student concession for third-class tickets on the 8:00 p.m. departure. It's packed, this time with penniless pilgrims, mostly men wearing loincloths whose faces are painted with yellow lines or at least with a rusty red forehead dot. We're all on our way to the Hindu holy city of Varanasi. Besides being a pilgrimage

Thumbs Out!

destination, it's an especially auspicious place to die, ensuring the departed an instant route to heaven. It is also a place to learn ancient Sanskrit and has had a special role in the development of Hindi, the national language of India.

We have to make a connection to get almost anywhere on the trains. After an hour, we change trains and pay the upcharge to get hard bed sleepers, using our usual bogus student discount.

After arriving in Varanasi at 1:30 p.m., we take a rickshaw to the government-run tourist bungalows. The place is fully booked, but they grant us the use of a room for the afternoon to shower and nap. On our way out to dinner, I convince the manager to extend our time until the morning. It's back to bed after another curry dinner.

On Friday, we're up early, fully rested and ready for another Indian onslaught. We leave the bungalows and walk to old Varanasi, finding the alleyways that lead to the Ganges River. They are winding, narrow, and dirty. We've been told that the best time to visit the west bank of the sacred Ganges River is in the early morning when you can see the pilgrims make their sin-cleansing dips in the river. We take a short boat ride to better view the scene.

The ghats are stairs that lead down to the river. There is a long strip of bathing ghats upstream from the two cremation ghats. The riverbanks are a swirl of religious activity. Women are bathing discreetly in saris, scooping up river water into jars to take home; men in loose-fitting clothes; face- and body-painted yogis; Brahmin priests offering blessings; and the ever-present beggars giving the pilgrims a chance for good karma. Everyone is marked with a red dot on their forehead after their ablutions. We see a dead baby floating in the water. Averting our eyes, we hope this scene is the last profoundly shocking reality on our morbidity tour.

Asia

After this boat ride, we wander the nearby crowded, narrow streets, which offer pilgrim-related services such as face-painting, safe storage for valuables by honest Brahmins seated under large straw umbrellas, flower necklace stalls, and open-air shops selling various colored cloths in which to wrap the dead.

The ritual bathing ghats in the Ganges River.

We follow the winding narrow alleyways to the Golden Temple, then to the Durga Temple, which is overrun with monkeys. We happen on an outdated outdoor relief map showing the contours of Greater India, from the British Colonialist perspective, showing the countries they ruled over: India, Pakistan, Nepal, Tibet, and Burma.

The weirdness continues when we encounter a small, random, white marble temple with strange, colorful, cartoonish wax figures scattered around the room. Most of the people are praying in front of a three-foot-square glass box in the middle of the room, in which sits a nameless, distorted wax man reading a book, the page moving back and forth mechanically. The box amplifies recorded popular Hindu music and has a swastika, the Hindu symbol for peace, painted on top, which the German Nazis borrowed as their symbol.

Thumbs Out!

We catch a bus to Sarnath, just six miles away from Varanasi, to visit one of India's major Buddhist centers. It was here that the Buddha preached his first sermon. In the local museum, we learn that he didn't want any statues idolizing him, but centuries later, statues of him in numerous postures abound around East Asia. Here, we also find the ancient ruins of the Ashoka Pillar, a statue that bears a wheel with twenty-four spokes, which represents the path to enlightenment. This symbol also appears in navy blue at the center of the Indian flag.

Back in Varanasi, we watch the sunset over the Ganges, have an early dinner, and go to bed as official residents of the government bungalows.

We get up early and take a rickshaw to the train station to buy our tickets to head to the Nepalese border the next night. We are deterred by the long, slow-moving line for third-class, so we upgrade to second-class.

Our rickshaw, passing some cargo-laden elephants, delivers us back to the Golden Temple, where we wander through the narrow alleyways again, this time heading toward the burning ghats. Two young wannabe guides fall in with us. Peter's morbid side is now exposed. He wants to see the cremations up close, so the boys guide us to a viewing platform overlooking a crematorium ghat. I'm a little queasy from the sweet, incense-laced smoke wafting up from the funeral pyres. The bodies are wrapped in cloths of different colors, depending on the sex and age of the deceased. The bodies of children under eight years old are simply deposited unburned into the Ganges.

We've chosen to experience this cultural overload and again we're hopeful these are our last encounters with dead bodies. The adult bodies are first dipped into the cleansing waters of the river on flimsy bamboo stretchers, after which the five-hour cremation process begins. As the ashes pile up, men comb through them, looking for gold or anything else of value left intact. Then the ashes are shoveled into the cleansing river.

After Peter has had his fix, we walk back to the bungalows, where we meet a Christian Indian couple who share bananas with us and tell us that their two brothers are living in Chicago, studying the Bible.

Religiously, culturally, and sensually overloaded, we climb into bed. This seems to confirm Peter's theory about religion: The spicier the food, the more vivid the dreams, the more colorful the religion.

The next day, we are ready to leave India. The train for the border with Nepal will leave at 8:00 p.m. There is only one second-class car and it's packed, so Peter buys discounted hard-bed sleeper tickets. The berths are so narrow that legs and arms are splayed into the aisle in this railcar rolling on a narrow-gauge track. We switch trains twice and finally arrive in Raxaul at 3:30 the next afternoon. From there, we take a rickshaw, pulled by the smallest horse we've ever seen, to the Indian border with Nepal.

Nepal

We enter Nepal at Birgunj. There are no trains in Nepal, so we find the local bus station to inquire about tickets for Kathmandu. The ticket counter clerk declares, "No more today, come back tomorrow." This delay suits me, since I feel like I've just been run over by a bus. I've felt increasingly tired and headachy for the past few days. It's a small town, and the only doctor we can find determines somehow that my problem

Thumbs Out!

is kidney-related and gives me a bottle of Pepto-Bismol. Peter convinces me not to take it. We find a hotel, and I fall into bed, thoroughly exhausted, while Peter goes out to dinner with a group of hippies we met on the train.

On Thursday, we're up early and return to the bus station. The buses are fully booked again. We look without luck for a bus alternative, then return to the station, where I plop on a bench while Peter reconnoiters then returns, telling me that he's arranged for bus passage without seats: We can sit in the aisle up front on our duffel.

"But my kidneys," I say.

He says, "I think it'll be okay."

We leave at 8:00 a.m. At our first stop, a kind fellow traveler offers us his bigger, softer duffel, making the trip up the verdant Himalayan foothills almost bearable. If I didn't feel so achy, I would be able to enjoy the zigzagging ride through vibrant green cultivated fields with accents of bright yellow mustard seed plants lining the road. As it happens, cloud cover obscures our first chance to see the Himalayas.

We arrive in Kathmandu at 6:00 p.m. and rickshaw to the recommended Kathmandu Lodge in the city center. Our fourth-floor room affords us a spectacular view of the Himalayas. I flop on the hard but clean bed for a while, then we walk down the street to the Dragon Restaurant for a so-so Tibetan dinner.

I spend the next day in bed. Peter brings me tea and toast in the morning, then wanders the colorful streets. A volley of gunfire from a military salute draws him into a street festival that, as he tells me later, was viewed by the king and queen from a platform. In the evening, we walk to a nearby restaurant and dine on a Nepalese specialty, *momo*—small, steamed dumplings filled with minced lamb, onions, chives, and spices, served with a sauce.

The next day, while taking a short walk around the neighborhood, I feel so exhausted that I retreat to rest in our room. Peter wanders around and reconnects with Zimmerman, a German traveler we had met in Teheran. The two of them spend the day together. I join them for brandy and another momo dinner. We return to the hotel, and I feel so cold that no amount of blankets can keep my teeth from chattering. Peter says adamantly, "We're going to see a real doctor tomorrow."

Friday morning, we ask the American Embassy for help finding a doctor. They direct us to the United Mission Hospital Tansen. We take a taxi up a hill to the hospital, which overlooks the city. We meet Dr. Dickinson, a tall Canadian, who examines me and takes X-rays, along with blood and urine samples. He is soft-spoken, gentle, and thorough. I'm so relieved to have this competent doctor helping me. Waiting for the results, I'm thinking, *Please, please figure out what this is so I can feel better.*

Finally, Dr. Dickinson returns and tells us that I have spinal meningitis. We sit in stunned silence, Peter's jaw dropping to the floor, he declares, considering the dire prognosis, "We'll fly back to the States."

But Dr. Dickinson replies, "You're not allowed on an airplane with spinal meningitis. But the good news is that we've found this strain of meningitis is far less dangerous than the usual Western types."

> **United Mission Hospital Tansen**
>
> It still sits on the same hill.

Thumbs Out!

Peter asks, "What's the next step?"

"Sally stays in the hospital, rests, and we do a spinal tap," Dr. Dickinson replies.

I'm admitted to the hospital, and Peter stays with me. He eventually leaves to find lunch, and Dr. Dickinson comes into my room with a large, empty syringe. He has me curl on my side in the fetal position, then he pokes the needle between the vertebrae in my spine. As he draws out my spinal fluid, I can feel the tension around my brain being sucked into the syringe. The relief is immediate. I'm so grateful and I tell him so.

He says, "Now you need to rest for a few days."

Peter returns and I tell him the good news. I can see how relieved he is, and we spend the afternoon figuring out our next steps. Peter stays all afternoon, has dinner with members of the hospital staff, and gets a ride back to the hotel with one of them.

The next morning, from my second-story hospital room, I gaze out my open window at the snow-capped mountains of the Himalayas filling the clear blue sky: Switzerland on steroids. I spot Peter riding a bicycle up the hill and call and wave. I look forward to his daily yarns. Today, after his ride, he tells me, "I rented this state-of-the-art, Indian-made, rickety, one-speed bike on Freak Street." Freak Street is the hippies' main artery, lined with countless hashish stalls and one bike shop. He continues, "One entrepreneurial hash vendor even advertises his hashish is the best because 'His Majesty recommends it.'"

On my third day in the hospital, Peter reports, "My state-of-the-art bicycle let me down. I was riding to Patan, only three miles away, and the front wheel fell off. I had to find a taxi to take me and my bike back to the bike shop in Kathmandu and get a replacement."

On day four, he tells me, "Today, I discovered that our only way forward is to fly to Bangkok. I am shopping around for a travel agent."

On day five, I'm going stir-crazy and ask to leave, but Dr. Dickinson thinks it's better I spend one more day here. Peter has kept his health insurance current, and the hospital agrees to accept his insurance coverage for all expenses. Peter's news today is, "I found Yeti Travel, owned by an Indian, who's willing to let us pay in Nepalese rupees, but I need your help to figure out our new itinerary."

On the sixth day, I pack my meager belongings into a small paper bag. Peter arrives on his bike after breakfast to pick me up. As we walk out the door with Dr. Dickinson, he warns Peter: "She still needs to rest for a few more days." But now he sees how his convalescing ex-patient is going to be transported home. With a wry smile, he joins my curious nurses, who have come to wave goodbye as I scooch onto the bicycle crossbar between Peter's arms, riding tandem. The ride down the hill into town is a little hairy, but beautiful.

Back at the Kathmandu Lodge, I rest a little, but I'm chomping at the bit, so Peter walks me over to Yeti Travel to introduce me to this disorganized, one-man operation. I find a phone-book-sized book sitting atop an empty desk and start paging through the Official Airline Guide (OAG). In it are all the timetables for every airline worldwide. I study the rules, taking over as the travel planner. I discover that it's best to stick to a specific airline, in this case, Pakistani International Airlines (PIA) and their partner airlines. This combination of airlines will get us all the way to Tokyo. Our imaginations take flight, finding places we want to see before we arrive in Tokyo.

I spend the next two days poring over the OAG. We design our itinerary with the idea of flying by the most circuitous route, with the most possible layovers between PIA flights as we make our way to Tokyo, the easiest place to get flights home. Peter is now looking to change his dollars into rupees at the best black market exchange rate so we can get a sweeter deal on the total cost of the flights that will take us to Japan.

In the meantime, Peter has also found the Meyers, an American couple who live here and want US dollars to travel with. They are offering him the best rate of exchange. The rupees can be obtained on the black market for at least three times the official exchange rate.

On Monday, October 17th, we take an air tour in a single-engine plane to see Mount Everest, paying for it with our black-market rupees. It's gloriously clear. We had been assuming that the tallest mountain in the world would stand out above all the other mountains. But Everest is not monolithic. It's one of many majestic peaks, just a bit higher than the rest.

Early in the day, I also rent a bike and ride with Peter through a smattering of rural life to Patan. Peter's newer "state-of-the-art" bike does not fall apart this time. Patan is loaded with ornate ancient architecture and artisanal shops that sell intricate wood and stone carvings.

Wednesday we visit one of the nearby Tibetan refugee camps where they weave rugs and sell them to support themselves. They fled the Tibetan uprising ten years ago, along with the Dalai Lama, and live here at a subsistence level. The Dalai Lama now lives in India in exile.

Asia

> **Kathmandu, Nepal**
>
> Hash (cannabis) has been illegal in Nepal since 1976. The country has a long history of use of cannabis for Ayurvedic medicine.

Finally, we board a bus to Kathmandu Airport. Our PIA flight to Bangkok via Dacca in East Pakistan is canceled. We are curious to see what compensation PIA will offer us as disrupted passengers. They put us up at the first-class Shanker Hotel in Kathmandu with food vouchers to eat at the hotel's fancy restaurant and a taxi to take us to the hotel. We have real hot showers for the first time since we left Istanbul.

We taxi back to the airport and board PIA's Boeing 707 flight to Dacca, along with only seven other passengers. We're in the cheap seats, but the food and service, including a small packet of five cigarettes, are first-rate. The flight is a little late, so our connection is tight. Our plan now morphs into missing the flight and getting put up by PIA. Along with Jack, a fun-loving English traveler on the same flight, we slow walk toward the gate for our next flight. A PIA worker catches on to our ploy and barks at us, "If you miss this flight, we will not put you up". The three of us transition to double time and make the departure for Bangkok.

Thailand

We're in Bangkok because of the geopolitics of Southeast Asia. In 1970, the Vietnam War is raging. We have no access to Burma, Laos, Cambodia, or Vietnam, which has created a virtual wall to overland travel. At Yeti Travel, the PIA rules and routes essentially dictated what will be our

Thumbs Out!

itinerary for the next two months—stops in Thailand, Malaysia, Singapore, Indonesia, Bali, and the Philippines, then a long stay in Japan before we head back home. But flying into Bangkok feels abrupt, and we're trading off some of our spontaneity with this new planned schedule. Now officially off the Hippie Trail, we rely even more on local information. We initially feel rudderless, but we embrace our chance to experience the new cultural variety of this final portion of our trip in Southeast Asia and Japan.

Almost immediately, it's apparent to us that Bangkok has become the go-to R & R destination for American GIs. Patpong Street, the city's most notorious hotspot for girlie bars, is overrun with soldiers on leave. Here, it's a cultural 180, in that there's little stigma about the openly sex-oriented bars, or, for that matter, being a sex worker. We've even been told by a Patpong patron about a proud father who boasted, "My daughter is so pretty that it's possible that she might become a whore someday."

> **Bangkok, Thailand**
>
> Patpong Street has evolved, but it is still a lively spot where cultures mix and nightlife thrives.

Thailand has a significantly higher standard of living and it's a better value for us travelers: hotels, food, and transport are clean, affordable, and well organized. We are still, per our modus operandi, choosing to eat at the usual crowded, Chinese-style restaurants and sleep in the ubiquitous low-cost city guest houses.

Pictures of the ever-so-popular king, King Bhumibol the Great, are everywhere, adorning restaurants, hotels, bars,

Asia

and billboards. He has no direct role in governing, but his influence is palpable. Every day at 8:00 a.m. and 6:00 p.m., we hear the Thai national anthem played on loudspeakers in the streets, on TV, on radio, and even on public transport. All the traffic and pedestrians stop and stand respectfully still. It is like a freeze-frame until the anthem ends and they resume their daily lives.

> **King Bhumibol**
>
> He reigned from 1946 to 2016. Between 1985 and 1994, Thailand was the world's fastest growing economy.

For four days, we stay at the good-value Atlantic Club hotel near the ancient temple area. English is seldom spoken, but in user-friendly Thailand, a well-organized, government-run travel assistance office network, called the Tourist Police, serves to orient us. We take water taxis to visit Wat Arun, Bangkok's oldest temple, depicted on the Thai currency, and Wat Pho, where the largest reclining Buddha, covered with gold leaf, resides next to a massage school. We catch the action on Patpong Street on two different nights. We attend a Thai boxing match that starts with a little dance by each boxer, followed by almsgiving, then mayhem: gloveless fists, bare feet, elbows, and knees flying. On another night, in a bar, we watch the Cassius Clay versus Jerry Quarry boxing match via satellite TV, a brand-new technology.

Since we booked our flight into Bangkok and our next flight out of Singapore, we're left with a welcome open-jaw land connection. We cavalierly sought orientation for this overland trip looking only at the small world globe back in the office of Yeti Travel; we never checked the actual distance on a map, assuming it couldn't be too far.

We take a bus to the outskirts of Bangkok to begin hitchhiking south to Malaysia, thinking we will sleep in Singapore tonight. After a few short rides, a Datsun pickup truck full of construction material, with four male passengers—two in the front seat and two in the back—stops and stuffs us into the back seat. The driver speaks English: "Well, we can take you to the Malaysian border. That's where we're going, and that'll take two days."

Peter inquires, "Exactly how far is it to Singapore?"

We can see the driver's eyes roll in the rearview mirror—around 1,300 miles. Peter looks at me: "OOPS."

We stop at a building site where we all have dinner with some of their fellow construction engineers and finally enjoy our first Thai food. We all sit outside at a big table under a tent. An electric cord swings from the top of a streetlight to our tent to provide power for the lights in the tent. We start with some Thai whiskey while a cook uses a wok to prepare our spicy Thai chicken curry. Once it's ready, the curry is served over rice. "Look what we've been missing," Peter says.

After dinner, we all pile back into the truck and drive until 10:00 p.m. We check into a typical Thai hotel, which is clean, affordable, and has a private bath with a hot shower.

Continuing on our road trip, we start early the next morning with a quick breakfast around 10:00. At this point, Peter insists on paying our own way from here on out since we shared dinner with them and no money was exchanged. We drive all day to Trang in southern Thailand, sometimes with a view of the sea, where we see many fishing boats and a tin mining operation on one desolate sandy beach.

Asia

Malaysia

The next morning, we reach our drivers' construction site at the Malaysian border and are off-loaded. There isn't much traffic as we wait for cars crossing into Malaysia. At a convenience store near the border, I spot a man removing his jacket as he prepares to get back into his Peugeot. I approach him and ask, "Can we get a ride with you south?"

Without hesitation, he says, "Come on," waving to Peter. "Let's go."

Peter sits in front and I'm in the back. The driver tells us he lives on Penang Island and is heading home. Peter suggests that it might be an interesting side trip, looking back to me for a nod.

Then the driver fills us in. "There was a bloody street clash between the Malays and the Chinese on the island in Georgetown City a year ago, but all is calm now."

We drive down the coast, then take a 20-minute ferry ride to Penang Island. Our driver drops us at an upscale hotel, but we find a cheaper one around the corner and decide to stay for two nights.

This is an affluent island dominated by Chinese Malaysians—Malaysian citizens of Chinese ethnicity like our driver. Throughout Malaysia, there is a rift simmering between the ruling rich minority Chinese Malaysians and the Malay majority citizens. Even if minority Chinese do not hold political sway, their financial dominance is a pattern we are seeing throughout Southeast Asia; and it's most pronounced here.

The next morning, we bus out to Batu Ferringhi, a beach northwest of Georgetown, and meander down the long, lonely, undeveloped beach. We bus back, walk the city streets, eat, and sleep.

We take a ferry back to the mainland and make our way to the highway heading south. We hitchhike with some overly speedy young drivers to the outskirts of Kuala Lumpur. Here we are picked up by Wong, a Chinese 20-something dressed in black. Wong is on his way to Singapore, now only about a four-hour drive away. He's gregarious and happy to have someone to talk to. He tells us, "My father recently died. That's why I have this patch on my left arm. Our entire family is in mourning, which means dressing in black, not shaving or cutting our hair. Now, I'm on my way to Singapore to reunite with all my family and I'll stay there for 30 to 100 days."

Peter interjects, "That sounds like a long time."

"Well, in ancient times, it was a thousand days."

Singapore

Wong drops us at the modest Hotel Central in Singapore. In the morning, we apply for our visas at the Indonesian Embassy, then go shopping. Yes, shopping. It's been our plan to buy a camera somewhere in Asia. Wong had advised us to choose a Chinese shop owner, since they are honest, rather than an Indian shop owner since he considered them a bit dodgy. Wong's ethnic pride registers as a gentle warning, but we still wish to keep our options open. After shopping around, we end up buying a 35mm Pentax camera from a Chinese shop after all.

Roaming around Singapore checking out camera shops, we find the city is modern and litter-free, filled with New York -style high-rise buildings; glitzy shops; and small, well-kept grassy parks. From a hilltop park, we can see hundreds of

Asia

Chinese junks, parked gunnel to gunnel, like a parking lot, off the shore of Singapore's Chinatown, where compact, one-story homes are smashed together.

When we ask Wong about restaurants, he tells us, "The place to go is Boogie Street, and be sure to have a drink at the famous Raffles Hotel bar." Since the local language is English, it's easy for us to ask for directions to Boogie Street. However, our inquiries elicit giggles, piquing our curiosity as we're pointed in the right direction. Boogie Street is lined with bars and restaurants with tables spilling out on the streets. We sit at a table and wonder what was so amusing when we asked people for directions to Boogie Street. There's a parade of provocatively dressed gorgeous women. Their sashaying seems to me to be a bit too theatrical, almost overly feminine. Stopping for a beer, we ask our server about these beauties.

"They are all boys," he replies.

Peter: "Aaah, now we get it."

> **Singapore**
>
> In Malay, the name is Bugis (Boogie) Street. In the mid-1980s, Bugis Street was redeveloped as a retail complex of modern shopping malls.

In the morning, we pick up our Indonesian visas and walk over to the American Express office to possibly pick up our mail from home. We're surprised that after giving our families only two weeks' notice of our dates in Singapore, letters have arrived. My mother-in-law, Viola, parses the Milwaukee weather. My mom peppers us with questions. Peter's brother Joe, a stockbroker, is all business. 1970 has been a harsh year for Peter's meager investments. Even the mail service is better here.

For the rest of the day, we stroll the streets of this sophisticated city. We do a walk-through of the Long Bar in the Raffles Hotel, with its posh wicker chairs and tables, then end up back on Boogie Street, where again we take in the local entertainment.

The next afternoon, we bus out to the airport and board our Garuda Airlines flight to Jakarta, Indonesia, the next stop on our Yeti Travel-designed itinerary. It seems to us that all the Asian airlines, including Garuda, offer impeccable service and food, even in the cheap seats.

Indonesia

We land in Jakarta at 4:30 p.m. All the hotels near the city's rail station are full, and our brief perusal of the city coming in from the airport has left us unimpressed, so we purchase tickets for the overnight train to Jogjakarta, in central Java, which departs at 6:30 p.m. This is our briefest layover ever in a city—only two hours. We might as well have flown straight to Bali, the next island to the east of Java in the Indonesian archipelago, since Bali is our next must-see destination.

We lay over in Jogjakarta, find a hotel for the night, take naps, and wait out the all-day rain. We're up early the next morning and catch a 4:55 train that takes us farther east to Surabaya. Since we are well rested, we watch the lush green rice paddies being tended by women in conical hats parading past our window. It's another brief visit in Surabaya, where we arrive at noon and book seats on the 9:30 night bus that will take us to Denpasar, the capitol of Bali Island. But we

Asia

give it our best shot, packing our short, rain-soaked stay with our last chance to experience Java.

We take a bemo, a Japanese-made three-wheeler with two passenger seats, to the local zoo. Java is so densely populated and cultivated, with almost every inch devoted to growing rice, that we don't see any animals in the wild, not even birds. At the entrance to this 37-acre zoo, we're issued umbrellas to view the animals that are outside. The aviary is overcrowded with almost too many colorful local birds. The highlight for us is the Komodo dragon, the biggest lizard in the world, which looks like a small dragon and comes from Komodo Island, located two islands east of Bali.

Later, before boarding our bus to Bali, we stop at the casino—yes, the casino. At the roulette table, Peter puts a 100-rupee bet on red, and he wins. One good bet, and we're out of there...winners.

The bus is another squirmy, restless, overnight ride, followed by a ferry crossing. Early the next day—a clear, sunny, and hot morning— we continue toward Denpasar, driving along the coast, with its views of neat, irrigated rice fields.

In Denpasar, Bali's capital city, we check into Hotel Irama for an eight-night stay. It's early, so we take two connecting bemos to Kuta beach, 12 miles outside of town. We're alone, overwhelmed by views of the wide, dramatic, crescent shaped coastline and the crashing waves that are soothed by the wide, white sand beach. Tall palm groves line the back edge of the beach, and above the trees, soaring green mountains rise up to the blue sky. *How can such a vast strip of beach still be so undeveloped and pristine?* We strip to our underwear and dive into the surf. We learn later that a Sheraton Hotel is about to be the first hotel on this beach.

Thumbs Out!

Back in Denpasar, we eat dinner for the first time at the Delicious Restaurant, an aptly named and renowned food factory. Peter devours his turtle steak, the must-have specialty of the house, and we waddle home to bed.

> **Bali, Indonesia**
>
> Kuta Beach became popular with surfers due to good wave conditions. In 2002, the Bali bombing occurred in October. Suicide bombers blew up Paddy's Pub and the Sari Club, killing 240 people, including 88 Australians.

Bali is the only Hindu-majority Island in Indonesia. But the Hinduism practiced here is not like the religion we saw in India. It brings together Indian Hindu gods with the island's animistic beliefs. Animism is the belief that objects, places, and creatures all possess a distinct spiritual essence. Also, people who subscribe to animism believe that their ancestors' souls are still around them in this world, and they worship their ancestors with offerings and ceremonies throughout the year. These beliefs create an atmosphere that is open to artists, ideas, celebrations, dance, and joy.

At Yeti Travel, as we planned an itinerary that would finally bring us back home to Milwaukee in December, studying our twisting and turning options, we'd always included time in Bali. One of our early thoughts was to island hop through the Indonesian archipelago to East Timor, then catch a ferry to Australia. But even this route included a layover in Bali.

And now that we're here, Peter proposes that in this year of travel, Bali is closer to Shangri-la than any place we've visited. Peter has rented a cheap motorbike. We make a broad loop along the coast, then climb up Kintamani, the highest mountain on the island. It's cold up here, especially when it

Asia

rains. In Kintamani Village, the clouds part for a while to expose Mount Batur, an active, smoking volcano. We descend to the green foothills with their intricately tiered rice paddies, spending one night in Ubud, an artists' enclave. Meandering around Ubud, we pass by the house of Antonio Blanco, the renowned resident Spanish artist born in the Philippines and collector of Balinese art, on our way to visit the Elephant Cave, an 11th-century cave where the entryway is carved like the mouth of a demon.

> **Ubud, Bali**
>
> A peaceful village with the wellness scene booming: Yoga schools, meditation centers, and vegan cuisine cooking classes.

Over the course of two days, we happen upon dance performances at four different temples. These elaborately choreographed temple dances tell Hindu stories, and they're part of everyday life here, attended by locals and the tourists who happen by.

On a return trip to Kuta Beach, the sun and heat require us to hydrate. There is one lonely lady vendor selling soda pop. As Peter quaffs his warm bottled drink, I can't resist the icy-cold option, drinking mine on ice. As the clock hands spin, the organisms multiply, and by evening, I'm down for the count. It's not a rare occurrence here, so Peter easily finds the magic pills that slowly win the fierce battle in my gut, but only after hours of agony.

Every morning, we eat a light breakfast on the veranda at the Irama Hotel with two English travelers, and each time, a friendly yet persistent peddler of carved wooden statues unpacks his wares, placing them around us. We can't help but show interest, since they're all beautifully carved out of the local heavy, dark hardwood.

Thumbs Out!

One of "twelop" statues.

Never intending to be a buyer, Peter entertains us by making lowball offers as the seller spreads out his inventory: 12 different Balinese-themed pieces depicting local peasants. Twelve is pronounced "twelop" by our seller, so we take up his pronunciation. With no interest in roughly doubling our baggage weight, Peter makes a super lowball offer for all twelop carvings. I can tell the seller is considering this offer because, for the first time, he stops his sales pitch and is quiet.

The next morning, our last in Bali, the seller once again hauls in his twelop carvings and surprises Peter by accepting the offer he made the previous day. A deal is a deal. We spend hours devising a way to package them for air travel.

Our two British breakfast buddies, Greg and Bob, are flying out on the same flight with us to Singapore the next morning. We four have our final dinner together at the Delicious.

Singapore, Thailand, Philippines

On Monday, we fly on Garuda Airlines back to Singapore, where we're put up at the Hotel Prince Garini, since our connection to Bangkok is leaving the next day.

It took a lot of maneuvering at Yeti Travel to arrange this misconnection. For once, we can help some fellow travelers

Asia

rather than having them help us. We offer a ride to Greg and Bob in our free taxi to our free hotel and invite them to use our bathroom and shower before they head to their overnight bus to Kuala Lumpur. We have meal vouchers and a frumpy, comfy room with all the amenities, so for once we stay in for the evening. Climbing into our king-size bed, we have a session of true confessions.

I start, "I think the jetsetters are lonely."

Peter says, "I think this is boring. Remember our honeymoon in Jamaica?"

In the morning, we have breakfast in bed, then do a bit of shopping before heading to the airport. Now we're starting to think about Christmas presents for the family, in addition to the twelop wooden statues we've already acquired. Our baggage will continue to grow. Flying on Thai Air, we connect to Bangkok via Kuala Lumpur.

After getting off the plane, with the usual spiffy service and food, we're a bit tipsy from the champagne. What have we become? Whisking through Singapore and now Bangkok sounded like fun when we were in Nepal, but in reality, it's just killing time for free. It's another lonely, first-class hotel room with food vouchers.

The following morning, we fly to Manila. Fortunately, we're allowed to ship our excess luggage directly to Tokyo. We won't be put up here by the airlines, since we've chosen to lay over for a few days. So, it's back to our old ways. We call the Peace Corps office for their hotel recommendation.

We have to hunt around to find the Methodist Guest House. English is widely spoken here in this Catholic country. I suppose the Catholics wouldn't know how to direct us to a Methodist guesthouse, but being able to communicate easily

Thumbs Out!

in English did help us get there. The wind picks up and it rains all night.

In the morning, Typhoon Yoling, aka Patsy, officially slams into Manila. Our guesthouse is one story, and we're watching the storm intensify outside our window when the roof of the two-story building across the street detaches and swirls into the sky. The guesthouse offers no food. When the wind dies down and the sky lightens up at around 1:00 p.m., we are in the eye of the storm. Peter takes this opportunity to look for some food. Moving fast, he finds an open sandwich shop and orders in relative tranquility. He is waiting for his order when the other side of the typhoon barrels in.

> **Manila, Philippines**
>
> Typhoon Patsy's damage was reported as $80 million, with 241 dead. Many more typhoons have hit the Philippines with higher death tolls. It's part of island life.

He returns soaked and windblown, carrying two soggy cheese sandwiches. He tells me, "I was still waiting when the wind hit again. I instinctively jumped over the service counter in one bound to find safety. I think it's the highest I've ever jumped in my life."

The winds slowly subside, and at twilight we venture out onto the streets, seeing big trees down, flooded streets, no electricity, and mostly closed-up storefronts. It seems there's always someone who's ready to serve food, so we dig up dinner down the street.

In the morning, we wander around, seeing more of the typhoon's devastation—a large cargo ship lies on its side on the beach, houses toppled, and streets blocked with debris. We're surprised to find the Japanese Embassy is open, and we

House across street where we saw the roof fly off.

pick up our visas. Manila has become resilient, since typhoons are a regular occurrence here. We drink warm local San Miguel beer and eat delicious chicken adobo by candlelight in a nearby restaurant.

On Saturday, all is calm, and the clean-up is in progress. Entering the airport terminal in a bus, we pass under the big picture of President Ferdinand Marcos. Our flight to Tokyo arrives after midnight, when almost everything is closed, so we just crash on benches in the airport.

Japan

On Sunday morning, we collect our forwarded baggage, bus into central Tokyo, and secure a room at the recommended Okubo House for a price that leads Peter to ask for a smaller room.

Thumbs Out!

"This is our most economical room, sir."

I find our room while Peter arranges for our expanded luggage to be stored. I see how small the room is, but Peter enters assuming our room is the entrance to a larger room. He takes two steps and extends his arm to open what he thinks is the door.

"Stop. That's the window, not a door. You are in the room." I can't help but smirk as he realizes he's already in the room, which is the size of two tatami mats. How do I know this? We put our bag in the closet and unfurl two tatami mats that fill the entire space, then we nap comfortably until noon.

As we leave, the owner admonishes us for being in the room between 9:30 a.m. and 5:30 p.m. since the room must be vacated during the day. We are catching on to the new arbitrary rules that are enforced by the General, as we now call him.

We take an overpacked subway to Ginza, Tokyo's famous shopping district. Neon signs cover every bit of space that isn't a door or a window, and their lettering is artwork in itself. Later we eat at a small inn that has plastic replicas of the dishes it serves displayed in the window.

When we return to the Okubo, I realize that I'm the only female staying here. There are two hot baths, one for men and one for women. Because these baths are communal, we must soap up and shower before entering the bath. Peter joins me in the empty women's hot bath to warm up. Since there's no central heating here, downstairs in a common room we sit on the floor at a low table with a space heater underneath. With our legs warm under the table, we exchange travel tales with the other English-speaking guests.

Asia

At 11:30 p.m. sharp, the General plays recorded chimes, then dictates his final instructions of the night: "It's time to go to bed. Please refrain from smoking and turn your lights out."

The next afternoon, we attend a Kabuki theatre, where the performers wear elaborate traditional costumes and extreme makeup and are prone to overly emotive acting—very long and drawn out. The audience yells and claps in approval or groans in disapproval of the complex plot turns. We slip out for breaks in the lobby a couple of times, then just give it up. It's an acquired taste.

I've recently discovered lice in my hair, so we try but fail to find medication. First of all, the ever-so-clean Japanese would never have lice, and the word rice is usually pronounced here as lice because they pronounce their Rs as Ls. Peter finds a can of OFF, the insect repellent. What's to lose?

Just before the General lays down the law, Peter sprays my hair with OFF. In the morning, I feel no lice in my hair. Multiple washes slightly help get some of the oil residue out, but the next day, the lice are back. The old lice died, but the eggs have hatched, and I'm back at square one.

We tour around Tokyo using the subways to visit museums, exhibits, the tourist office, and the famous Mikimoto pearl shop to buy pearls for our moms and my French mama in Calais.

On Thursday, we take the subway out of the city to hitch to Kyoto. Every tidy acre has something on it: factories, crops, or small gardens. This area is reputed to be the most populated in all of heavily populated Japan. It has always seemed to us that, throughout the world, higher population density leads to higher crime. But not here. Japan is virtually crime-free. Throughout our travels, we've always heeded any local warnings of danger. You can always tell how pressing the warnings are by their tone of voice. It's served us well. In addition to this heads-up messaging, the *lack* of any mention of crime has let us know when we are good to go.

We check into Hotel Sakasta House in Kyoto, and for the first night, we're relegated to the sleeping dormitories, where we meet Linda and Hiro, our bunkmates. Fortunately, we're able to procure private rooms for the rest of our stay, but we're also happy to spend time with Linda and Hiro. Hiro was born in Japan but now lives in California with Linda. They invite us to join them for sightseeing. First, though, Hiro helps me buy some delousing shampoo that actually works.

We've rarely stayed in one city for a whole week, or in a single country for more than twenty days. For various reasons, we've spent longer blocks of time in Mexico, Ecuador, Peru, France, Turkey, and Nepal. And now we plan to spend almost a month in Japan.

Hiro will be our guide in and around Kyoto for the next few days. He shows us the fall colors of tiny, crimson-leafed Japanese maples, the Golden Temple, the city's famous rock garden, bonsai exhibitions, and sumo wrestling on TV. He also introduces us to sake, sushi, and chopsticks instructions and takes us on a day trip to Nara to see the world's largest freestanding Buddha statue and the Imperial Palace, with its 300-year-old garden. The Japanese gardens are unique in their simplicity, lacking flowers and placing emphasis on nature. My favorite is the Contemplative Garden, where a few large rocks sit on a sea of manicured sand.

During our stay in Kyoto, we celebrate our first-year anniversary on November 29th. Peter, that old romantic, suggests a couple of beers and sushi. I hold out for the Hechima Inn, a traditional Japanese ryokan.

Kyoto – Ryoanji Temple Rock Garden, UNESCO World Heritage site.

We check in, taking off our shoes. We are shown to our large, simple room, with a separate sleeping room with tatami mats laid out. We have our own hot bath with a view of the colorful trees. We wash up and sit in the bath, then put on kimono robes, sipping sake while waiting for dinner.

Peter suggests, "Shouldn't this be about our fifth anniversary? I mean, we've spent 24 hours a day together since we left Milwaukee."

After dinner, we go out for a long walk, returning later to sleep on the same type of tatami mats that the General has. Little did I know that in Tokyo, we were staying in a Japanese ryokan all along.

We get back on the road, heading to our next destination, Hiroshima, where the *Enola Gay* bomber dropped the atomic bomb 25 years ago. On the highway outside of Kyoto, Tedsan and his friend Smiley (my name for him) pull over to pick us up, offering us a ride in the wrong direction and presenting us with another split-second decision that we decide to accept.

Tedsan speaks English, and not long after exchanging short versions of our stories, he proposes a one-week job for us in his hometown. He lives in the small city of Nagahama on the shores of Lake Biwa. His uncle is opening a new Western-themed restaurant there, and he'd like us to act as a chef and a head waitress during the restaurant's opening week to bring it some credibility. We immediately express our enthusiasm for this plan, dropping the idea of visiting Hiroshima. It's the start of a gig that never happens, but even though the plan—with the promise of employment and the chance to be stars—eventually falls apart, the ride we take with Tedsan, literally and figuratively, will entertain us for days.

On the way to Nagahama, Tedsan has to make a stop in Osaka, so we leave our duffel in his car, establish a time and place to meet two hours later, and set out for a walk around downtown Osaka. We return to our appointed meeting place on time, but Tedsan is late to pick us up. After waiting for an hour, we're worried, imagining that this was all a ruse, trying to figure out what to do next. We're contemplating calling the police when he finally shows up an hour and a half after our set meeting time. We'd just assumed that all Japanese are not only honest but also punctual.

We have been on the road for nearly a year. Now in Japan, we are impressed with the lack of crime just like we experienced in England six months ago. All along our route, we have been aware of the potential to be victims of the ever-present thieves and robbers, except in these two island nations, one in the Atlantic and one in the Pacific.

Peter says," I could randomly hand my wallet to anyone on the street here and request to meet up the next day and

Asia

they would be there, my wallet in hand." Call it the concept of honor. Japan and England still live this way and their influence on the rest of the world has at least rubbed off a little. We have had almost no crime issues but we're thankful for the influence of these national rocks, one off Europe and one-off Asia. The downside is that honor can be manifested in militarism or colonialism, but for us, it's a pleasure to proceed with relaxed vigilance.

From Osaka, it's a short trip north to Nagahama. Tedsan takes us to his small, simple home, where his mother serves the three of us dinner. Then we go to meet his uncle, our new boss, at his office. The sake is brought in as the negotiations begin. We will start on December 8th and work one week until December 15th, with room and board as part of our compensation. Peter, enthralled with this "out of the box" offer, discards his usual role as the tough negotiator, says, "The pay is up to you and not important." We can't wait.

We sleep in the living room at Tedsan's, feeling as if we're depriving someone in this household of blankets and pillows. His sweet mother makes us breakfast in the morning, and then Tedsan takes us to another meeting scheduled for 10:00 a.m. that starts at noon. Next, we're taken to a photographer's studio and presented with a chef's outfit and a waitress's uniform. Luckily, I fit into the largest size they have. Promotional photos are taken, and then Tedsan drives us to the highway and drops us off to hitch back to Tokyo.

We arrive back at the Okubo House around 9:30 p.m. We'll kill three days in Tokyo before our gig in Nagahama starts on the 8th. We hook up again with Linda and Hiro.

On Monday, by chance the day that will live in infamy, December 7th, we have to prepare for our flight to Honolulu on the evening of December 15th, because we'll be working all

Thumbs Out!

week and leaving Nagahama right after work that day. The next day, we hitch back to Nagahama to meet in the boss's office at 6:00 p.m. We're told that a snowstorm has damaged the restaurant and delayed the opening until the 17th. So our gig just goes poof.

But the boss and his whole team, including Tedsan, want to make it up to us, starting now. So let the party begin. They book us a luxurious room at the best hotel in town and rent a meeting room in the hotel for our sorry-about-that fete, inviting about 20 team members, including the restaurant's general manager, architect, the boss, interpreters, some of Tedsan's friends, and the real chef. They present a framed photo of us in our waitress and chef outfits and give us a discreet envelope with 10,000 Japanese yen. In the Japanese style, the food and drink never, never end. Finally, back in our hotel room, we find more food and drinks laid out for us.

Peter and Sally in a promotional photo for a new Japanese restaurant.

The next day, the general manager and architect take us to breakfast, then sightseeing, and to a nine-course trout lunch in a trout farm restaurant. We have our bag in their car, so after lunch, around 3:30 p.m., they drive us to the highway and drop us off to hitch to Tokyo. A cold, blustery wind brings us back to reality, but soon we're picked up by an older man and taken to his house in the Tokyo suburbs. He invites us into his house and feeds us some hot soup. Then he has his daughter, after already gifting me a necklace, drive us to the subway. Still a bit dazed by our days of twists and turns, we're back at the Okubo House by 9:00 p.m.

There we meet Chris, a Kiwi architect and fellow guest. The next day, he takes us around to view buildings designed in interesting ways, one of which looks like a battleship, painted silver. From its roof, it feels just like we are on the deck of a ship.

We change our plane tickets to leave for Honolulu on December 11th. Tokyo is becoming a small town to us. Our eyes are starting to glaze over, and it's too cold. Having piled up our baggage with Christmas gifts for the family, Peter makes one last purchase for his brother, Joe—a secondhand pachinko machine. Pachinko, a kind of pinball game, is all the rage here, and we have taken to playing it. We make a simple, straightforward purchase from our local pachinko parlor, and now our luggage can fill a van. With mixed emotions, we're homeward bound.

For our last meal, on our last night in Tokyo, we join a group from the Okubo House, including Linda and Hiro, to eat at a restaurant where whale meat is the specialty. To me, it looks like blubber and tastes like liver.

Back at the Okubo, the General sends us to bed for the last time. On Friday, December 11th, we fill a taxi with our stuff and head to the monorail that serves the airport. We have lots of time at the airport before Linda and Hiro join us to see us off and put the final touch on our luggage heap: four suitcases that they've asked us to take to San Francisco for them. Per our agreement, they pay the excess luggage charge of a hundred dollars. Linda and Hiro give us our first in-person goodbye since Mama and Papa waved us off in Calais.

USA

In Honolulu, we're just simple tourists soaking up the warmth, sun, and surf at Waikiki Beach for four days.

In San Francisco, where we spend the next four days, it's the same, but colder. In a coffee shop sitting across from each other, I say, "I think I remember every day of my life in 1970."

"What about 1969?" Peter puts his hand on the table and wiggles his fingers and I take it in for a squeeze.

"At least, I remember our wedding day."

Arriving in Milwaukee on December 20th, we complete the circle. It's a whirlwind of family, fun, friends, and questions over the holidays. On the day after Christmas, we wake up at my parents' house in my old bedroom.

I ask Peter, "Is there anything on our schedule today?"

"We have a clean slate."

"We really have a clean slate forever."

"Nothing."

Silence.

"I guess we need to make plans," I say.

"Let's make a list," Peter says. "We need a place to live, and to figure out where that will be. We need a car. Gotta make a living. Do we have any money? And clothes to wear?"

"Let's enjoy every day, but in a new way."

On New Year's Eve, 1970, after settling in for a few days, I wistfully say to Peter, as midnight approaches, "Someday I want to see Africa."

"Me too."

"Let's look at a map."

"No. Let's go over to the UWM library and spin the globe."

About the Authors

Peter and Sally Blommer were both born and raised in Milwaukee, Wisconsin, and still live there to this day. Peter graduated from Georgetown University and Sally graduated from the University of Wisconsin-Milwaukee (UWM). Peter had been a high-school classmate of Sally's brother, so they knew each other. They reconnected when she was 23 and he was 28 years old. They dated and married on November 29, 1969. As newlyweds, they hitchhiked around the world in 1970 for a year.

After their one-year world trip, Peter went into business, opening a chain of restaurants. Sally worked as a travel agent and later started her own agency.

After their 1970 world trip, they felt they couldn't capture the feeling of the close-to-the-ground travel until they discovered bicycle touring. They started a website, www.ridetheroad.com and maintained it for more than 30 years. They graded the countries biked in and reported on where to find the best biking in the world. Peter and Sally spent four months a year on the road, so after three decades, they had completed the equivalent of ten years bicycle-traveling all around the world, always trying to beat the crowds to the exceptional destinations.

During the Covid pandemic, they spawned the idea of writing a book about their 1970 world trip. Fifty-five years later, it reads like history.

Thumbs Out is their first book. With the many bicycle trips they have taken over the past 40 years worldwide, and Sally keeping daily diaries, they are now working on their next book about their bicycle adventures.

www.ingramcontent.com/pod-product-compliance
Lightning Source LLC
Chambersburg PA
CBHW050032090426
42735CB00022B/3454